# ROMANS

## Also by Tara-Leigh Cobble

*The Bible Recap:*
*A One-Year Guide to Reading and Understanding the Entire Bible*

*The Bible Recap Study Guide:*
*Daily Questions to Deepen Your Understanding of the Entire Bible*

*The Bible Recap Journal:*
*Your Daily Companion to the Entire Bible*

*The Bible Recap Discussion Guide:*
*Weekly Questions for Group Conversation on the Entire Bible*

*The Bible Recap Kids' Devotional:*
*365 Reflections and Activities for Children and Families*

*The God Shot:*
*100 Snapshots of God's Character in Scripture*

*Israel:*
*Beauty, Light, and Luxury*

*The Bible Recap for Kids:*
*A 365-Day Guide Through the Bible for Young Readers*

THE BIBLE RECAP KNOWING JESUS SERIES*

*Knowing Jesus as King:*
*A 10-Session Study on the Gospel of Matthew*

*Knowing Jesus as Servant:*
*A 10-Session Study on the Gospel of Mark*

*Knowing Jesus as Savior:*
*A 10-Session Study on the Gospel of Luke*

*Knowing Jesus as God:*
*A 10-Session Study on the Gospel of John*

THE BIBLE RECAP KNOWING GOD SERIES*

*Acts:*
*The Spirit and the Bride—a 10-Week Bible Study on God and His Church*

*General editor

# ROMANS

## DEAD TO SIN
## AND ALIVE TO CHRIST

### A 10-WEEK BIBLE STUDY

## TARA-LEIGH COBBLE,
### GENERAL EDITOR

#### WRITTEN BY THE D-GROUP THEOLOGY & CURRICULUM TEAM

BETHANYHOUSE

a division of Baker Publishing Group
Minneapolis, Minnesota

© 2025 by Tara-Leigh Cobble

Published by Bethany House Publishers
Minneapolis, Minnesota
BethanyHouse.com

Bethany House Publishers is a division of
Baker Publishing Group, Grand Rapids, Michigan

Printed in the United States of America

ISBN 9780764243615 (paper)
ISBN 9781493446926 (ebook)

Library of Congress Cataloging-in-Publication Control Number: 2024051124

The D-Group Theology & Curriculum Team is Emily Pickell, Abbey Dane, Kirsten McCloskey, Emma Dotter, Liz Suggs, Laura Buchelt, and Tara-Leigh Cobble.

The general editor is represented by Alive Literary Agency, AliveLiterary.com.

Interior design by Nadine Rewa
Cover design by Dan Pitts
Author image from © Meshali Mitchell

Baker Publishing Group publications use paper produced from sustainable forestry practices and postconsumer waste whenever possible.

25  26  27  28  29  30  31      7  6  5  4  3  2  1

# CONTENTS

# INTRODUCTION

The apostle Paul's missive to the believers in Rome is the first of twenty-one letters in the New Testament. We call these "epistles"—letters from an apostle. Paul wrote Romans during his third missionary journey in Corinth, around AD 58.

When Paul wrote to Rome, he hadn't visited the city yet, and Scripture doesn't tell us how the message of Christ had found its way there. As the center of the Roman Empire, Rome had a large population of Jews, so it's no surprise that such a large, diverse city included believers in Jesus.

Paul had a deep desire to visit the believers in Rome, but he wrote them this epistle in case he never had the chance to get there. Unlike many of Paul's other letters, his message to the Roman Christians doesn't focus on specific issues unique to their local church. Instead, he uses most of the letter to talk about humanity's pitfalls and God's redemptive plan. Church history tells us Paul eventually did make it to Rome and was martyred there.

The impact of Romans on Christianity cannot be overstated. Many of its passages have far-reaching implications for the everyday lives of believers. For generations, faithful men and women have discussed and debated Paul's theological points and have often come to vastly different conclusions. Despite the varied views people hold in response to Paul's words, it's important to remember that the letter is meant to point Christ-followers toward unity and clarity, not division and confusion.

This study is an opportunity to wrestle with difficult passages, to research what you don't understand, and to ask your questions! It's possible you may wrestle but not reach a full conclusion about a given topic— *and that's okay*. A humble willingness to grow in understanding can be immeasurably helpful in the process of learning more. Be prepared for the Holy Spirit to introduce different ways of thinking about your faith.

During this study, you will look very closely at the text, but don't forget to zoom out and remember the context of the whole letter. Doing so will help prevent us from building entire doctrines out of single verses.

Romans is full of major themes centered around Paul's systematic reasoning that righteousness comes from God through faith in Christ alone. One recurring theme is the role of the Mosaic law for those who are already saved. Should believers keep the law? Is it the law that provides salvation? Does keeping the law cause God to love us more?

*Luther's Small Catechism with Explanation* says this about the topic, "First, the Law helps to control violent outbursts of sin and keeps order in the world (a curb). . . . Second, the Law accuses us and shows us our sin (a mirror). . . . Third, the Law teaches us Christians what we should and should not do to live a God-pleasing life (a guide). The power to live according to the Law comes from the Gospel."[1] Pay close attention to what Paul says about the Holy Spirit; He seems to be the key to understanding the role of the law!

Paul also addresses issues that continue to impact the church today. Among these are the importance of unity of the body in the midst of a diverse culture, the doctrines of election and God's sovereignty, obedience to government, spiritual gifts, and the complexities of Christian liberties.

The apostle Peter says this about Paul in 2 Peter 3:16, "There are some things in [Paul's letters] that are hard to understand, which the ignorant and unstable twist to their own destruction, as they do the other Scriptures." So as you read, study, and wrestle, be encouraged that even Peter found Paul hard to understand sometimes!

# HOW TO USE THIS STUDY

While Bible study is vital to the Christian walk, a well-rounded spiritual life comes from engaging with other spiritual disciplines as well. This study is designed not only to equip you with greater knowledge and theological depth, but to help you engage in other formative practices that will create a fuller, more fulfilling relationship with Jesus. We want to see you thrive in every area of your life with God!

## Content and Questions

In each of the ten weeks of this study, the teaching and questions are divided into six days, but feel free to do it all at once if that's more manageable for your schedule. If you choose to complete each week's study in one sitting (especially if that time occurs later in the study-week), keep in mind that there are aspects you will want to be mindful of each day: the daily Bible reading, Scripture memorization, and the weekly challenge. Those are best attended to throughout the week.

## Daily Bible Reading

The daily Bible reading corresponds to our study. It will take an average of three minutes per day to simply read (not study) the text. If you're an auditory learner, you may prefer to listen to an audio version of these Bible chapters.

Even if you decide to do the week's content and questions in one sitting, we still encourage you to make the daily Bible reading a part of your regular daily rhythm. Establishing a habit of reading the Word every day will help fortify your faith and create greater connection with God.

If you decide to break the study up into the six allotted days each week, your daily Bible reading will align with your study. Days 1–5 will follow our study of Romans, Day 6 features a psalm that corresponds to our reading, and Day 7 serves as a catch-up day in case you fall behind.

## Scripture Memorization

Memorizing Scripture isn't busywork! It's an important part of hiding God's Word in our hearts (Psalm 119:11). Our memorization passage— Romans 8:1–11—focuses on our freedom from sin and death and our new life in Christ, via the presence of His Holy Spirit. We encourage you to practice it cumulatively—that is, *add* to what you're practicing each week instead of *replacing* it. We quote the English Standard Version (and some of our resources are in that translation as well), but feel free to memorize it in whatever translation you prefer. We suggest working on each week's verse(s) throughout the week, not just at the last minute. We've provided some free tools to help you with this, including a weekly verse song: MyDGroup.org/Resources/Romans.

## Weekly Challenge

This is our practical response to what we've learned each week. We want to be "doers of the word, and not hearers only" (James 1:22). You'll find a variety of challenges, and we encourage you to lean into them all—especially the ones you find *most* challenging! This will help strengthen your spiritual muscles and encourage you in your faith. As with the memory verse, you'll want to begin this practice earlier in the week, especially because some weekly challenges include things to do each day of the week (e.g., prayers, journaling, etc.).

## Resources

This is a Scripture-heavy study, and you'll find yourself looking up passages often. If you're new to studying Scripture, this will be a great way to dig in and sharpen your skills! You will feel more equipped and less intimidated as you move through each chapter. Some questions may ask you to refer to a Bible dictionary, commentary, or Greek or Hebrew lexicon, but you don't need to purchase those tools. There are lots of free options available online. We've linked to some of our favorite tools—plus additional resources such as podcasts, articles, and apps—at MyDGroup .org/Resources/Romans.

## Groups

Because each week has a lot of questions in the content, we offer the following recommendation for those who plan to discuss the study in a weekly group meeting. As each member is doing their homework, we suggest they mark their favorite items with a star and mark any confusing items with a question mark. This serves as preparation for the group discussion and helps direct the conversation in beneficial ways. Group leaders, please note the starred prompts in each chapter; we've highlighted these for you as topics you may find helpful to prioritize in group discussions.

┌─ Scripture to Memorize ─┐

There is therefore now no
condemnation for those
who are in Christ Jesus.

Romans 8:1

# Romans 1–2

*Note: If you haven't yet read How to Use This Study on pages 9–11, please do that before continuing. It will provide you with a proper framework and helpful tools.*

## DAILY BIBLE READING

Day 1: Romans 1:1–7

Day 2: Romans 1:8–17

Day 3: Romans 1:18–32

Day 4: Romans 2:1–11

Day 5: Romans 2:12–29

Day 6: Psalm 106

Day 7: Catch-Up Day

**Corresponds to Day 341 of *The Bible Recap*.**

## WEEKLY CHALLENGE

See page 40 for more information.

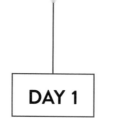

# Romans 1:1–7

### ✝ READ ROMANS 1:1–7

In ancient cultures, letter writers began their correspondence with a signature, a recipient, and a short greeting. Typical introductions would've sounded something like this: *Tara-Leigh Cobble. To Bible readers. Hey!* Or in the context of Romans, it might have said: *Paul. To Roman Christians. Hello.*

But here in the longest of his surviving letters, Paul didn't stick to the typical introduction. Instead, in seven verses containing one sentence (depending on what translation you read), Paul began with a multitude of theological truths.

**Review 1:1.**

1. Complete the chart below. Who did Paul say he was?

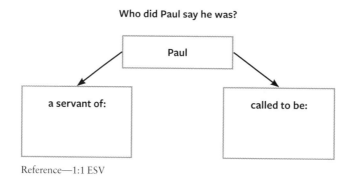

Who did Paul say he was?

Paul

a servant of:

called to be:

Reference—1:1 ESV

The Greek word used here for "servant," *doulos*, is closer in meaning to the English word *slave*. Understandably, it's difficult to grasp Paul's meaning here, because *slavery* in our context brings to mind depraved systems of enslavement prevalent around the world both now and in the not-too-distant past. But this word in that day's context didn't refer to an unwilling or forced obedience. Rather, it meant *complete* obedience.

2. **Use a Greek lexicon to look up the word for "apostle" (1:1).** What is it? What does it mean?

From the first words of his letter, Paul defined himself by Christ. And the rest of Paul's introduction wasn't about who he was, but about who Christ was—and *is*.

**Review 1:2–3.**

3. Complete the chart below. What was Paul set apart for?

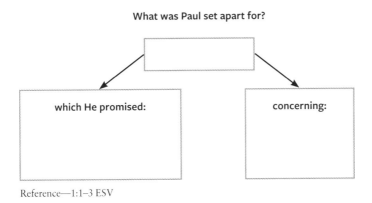

Reference—1:1–3 ESV

The gospel is God's good news for a broken and dying world, through His Son, Jesus Christ. It was planned from the beginning and promised throughout Scripture (Genesis 12:3; Isaiah 11:1; Zechariah 9:9–11). Every bit of God's Word—the Law and the Prophets, the Old Testament and the New—must be understood through the good news of God's Son.

**Review 1:4.**

4. Complete the chart below about the identity of God's Son.

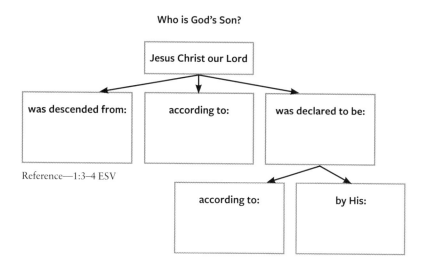

Who is God's Son?

Jesus Christ our Lord

was descended from:

according to:

was declared to be:

Reference—1:3–4 ESV

according to:

by His:

5. **Use a Greek lexicon to look up the word for "declared" (1:4).** What is it? What English word came from it? (Hint: What does the Greek word sound like?)

The same God who marked out where the land would stop and determined where the sky would begin also ordained His Son to be both lowly— condescending to our humanity in His life—and mighty—defeating death itself.

**Review 1:5.**

6. Complete the chart below about the gifts of Jesus.

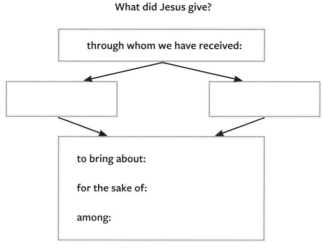

**What did Jesus give?**

through whom we have received:

to bring about:

for the sake of:

among:

Reference—1:5 ESV

Theologians differ in their interpretation of the "we" in 1:5. Some think Paul meant only himself. Some think he meant the recipients of his letter, Roman Christians. Some think he meant himself and other early church leaders. And some think he meant all believers, for all time. The interpretation of the word *we* in 1:5 can also impact your understanding of the word *apostleship*. Some theologians say all believers can be called apostles. Some say only a few leaders can be called apostles. And some say only the apostles of the first-century church (the twelve apostles plus Paul) held that title.

As we discussed in the introduction, faithful Christians can search and study God's Word and seek the Spirit's guidance and come to different conclusions about many topics. (If you haven't read the introduction yet, take a few minutes to do that now. As we get further into Romans, you'll be glad you did.)

**Review 1:6.**

★ 7. Who is definitely addressed in the "you" here? Who might also be included?*

Paul greeted his letter recipients, who lived in the center of an empire known not only for its military power, but also for its achievements in philosophy, science, literature, and art. Paul didn't greet them with platitudes about how smart or important they were. Much like how he introduced himself, Paul defined them by Someone other than themselves.

**Review 1:7.**

8. Complete the chart below about Paul's letter recipients.

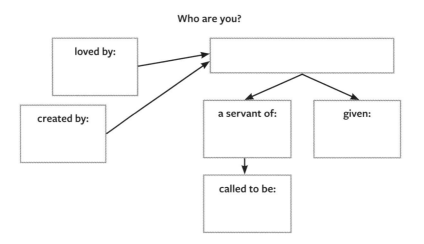

The word *saint* means holy and set apart. Paul didn't tell the Roman Christians they would be saints when they died; he said they were already saints. And if you're a follower of Christ today, *you're a saint too*. You are loved by God, and you're a recipient of grace and peace from God our Father and from the Lord Jesus Christ. Amen!

\* Starred prompts are specifically designed to be useful for group discussion.

★ 9. Review Paul's introduction and count the number of times he wrote "called," "set apart," and "promised beforehand." What does this tell you about a major theme in Romans?

# Romans 1:8–17

 **READ ROMANS 1:8-17**

In four parts, Paul began to wrap up his personal greeting to the Roman Christians, basically telling them: *"I thank God for you. I pray for you. I want to visit you. I've tried to visit you."*

**Review 1:8.**

1. Fill in the blanks in 1:8 below. Who did Paul thank for the Romans' faith? Through whom? These details are important—don't miss them!

I thank _____ _____ through _____ _____ for all of you, because your faith

is proclaimed in all the world.

Gratitude is a healthy practice, and it can be perspective shifting for anyone. But for the believer, gratitude (to the Father, through the Son) is a vital, heart-shaping practice.

**Review 1:9–10.**

For the second time in eight verses, Paul shined a spotlight on the gospel. Throughout Romans—and his other letters—Paul kept coming back to God's good news for a broken and dying world. It seems he felt the profound significance and the incomparable beauty of the gospel to the very core of his being. May God give us that same conviction.

2. According to 1:9–10, what did Paul mention every time he prayed? What was the heart behind his ceaseless prayer?

**Review 1:11–12.**

As we discussed in the introduction, Paul hadn't yet been to Rome when he wrote to the believers there. But he'd heard about their faithful, growing community, and longed to visit them—not just to encourage them, but to be encouraged by them. As one of the first Christian ministers, Paul understood the importance of mutual upbuilding: Service and encouragement flow both ways. Today, burnout among Christian ministers is all too common, and it might be tied to our failure to recognize ministry as a two-way street.

★ 3. If you work in ministry, list some ways you've been ministered to by those you serve. If you don't work in ministry, list some ways you can serve those who minister to you.

**Review 1:13–15.**

As Paul wrapped up his greeting, he emphasized that his ministry wasn't just to Jews, but to non-Jews (Gentiles) as well. He was appointed to minister to Greeks and to barbarians* (non-Greeks). He told the Romans that—despite his desire—he had so far been unsuccessful in his attempts to get to Rome. We now know Paul did eventually go to Rome, but when he was writing this letter, he wasn't sure he'd make it there. Even though he would arrive in Rome as a prisoner and shipwreck survivor, God answered Paul's prayer with a yes: Paul would preach the gospel in Rome (Acts 28:30–31).

**Review 1:16.**

For Paul to write that he wasn't ashamed of the gospel was an understatement. This was a man who had been attacked, chased out of town, and stoned for the sake of the gospel. He would soon be arrested, tried, and imprisoned. Eventually, he would be martyred. When Paul's devotion to the gospel was met with opposition, mockery, and even persecution, he didn't waver from the good news. The good news (gospel) doesn't promise salvation from our earthly struggles; it promises an eternal rescue from the penalty of our sins into relationship with God through the finished work of Jesus! And only by God's almighty power—which created the universe and everything in it, which defeated death, and which gives believers His indwelling Spirit—is salvation possible.

4. According to 1:16, who receives salvation? What does that reveal about the heart of God?

**Review 1:17.**

*When Paul referred to the non-Greeks as "barbarians," he wasn't insulting them. At the time, *barbarian* referred to anyone who didn't speak Greek. It wasn't until later in history that the word came to be used as a derogatory term.

To understand Paul's meaning in the final verse of today's section, a quick look at the prepositions is helpful. The English translation "righteousness of God" (1:17) is better understood as "righteousness *from* God." It's our right standing before God, given to us by God. He gives us the righteousness of His Son. Righteousness is His requirement, which only He can achieve and impart. *He does the doing*, and we get to enjoy our status because of Him.

And that righteousness is revealed "from faith for [*eis*] faith" (1:17). The preposition *eis* gives us insight into Paul's meaning, which is close to "from faith, into faith, to faith."

This idea encapsulates three aspects of how our relationship with Jesus transforms us. Theologians use three terms to help us clarify and understand what God accomplishes on our behalf. Because we'll see these words and themes throughout Romans, let's develop a basic understanding of them here.

★ 5. **Use a Bible dictionary to fill in the table below.** To complete the last column, make a personal connection to Paul's explanation of faith.

| This . . . | Points to . . . | Which means . . . | And this tells me . . . |
|---|---|---|---|
| From faith | Justification | | Ex: This one-time moment is just the beginning of our faith |
| Into faith | | | |
| To faith | Glorification | | |

Through Jesus, we received God's salvation by faith. We live by faith, guided by the Spirit. And one day, our faith will be made complete and we'll live with Him in His kingdom forever. Praise God for His gift of faith!

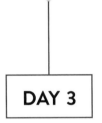

# Romans 1:18–32

## † READ ROMANS 1:18–32

**1. Write the definitions of *wrath* given by the sources listed below.**

A web search:

A Bible dictionary:

To the world, wrath seems like unrighteous anger, because most of the anger we see in the world is unrighteous. But God's wrath is always righteous. Before we study today, it's important to know that because Jesus absorbed all the Father's wrath for our sins during His death on the cross Christians won't experience God's wrath, *so take heart!* It's also important to remember that because of our sin God's wrath is what we deserve, *so stay humble.*

**Review 1:18.**

Until the middle of our next week in this study, we'll be studying the bad news. If the next few days of reading seem dark, it's because sin is dark. Sin is deadly serious and leaves us in dire need of a life-saving cure. If we take sin lightly, we'll take our salvation lightly.

But Paul's writings on man's sin and God's wrath fall between his writings on the cure.

2. Reread 1:17 and preview 3:22 below. Circle the phrases they have in common.

"The righteousness of God is revealed from faith for faith, as it is written, 'The righteous shall live by faith'" (1:17).

"...the righteousness of God through faith in Jesus Christ for all who believe" (3:22).

The bad news is sandwiched between the best news: Christians are righteous before God because He made us righteous. So let's lean into the bad news so we can more fully understand, cling to, and praise God for the good news.

Throughout the next few sections of Scripture (1:18–3:31), Paul addressed four different types of people with unique (but related) problems. You'll see that he followed a similar pattern in each section, essentially explaining that each group *knows who God is, but hasn't responded appropriately to that knowledge, continuing in their sin, and are therefore deserving of God's wrath.* All four categories of people—which included both Jews and Gentiles—have sinned, and all are in equal need of salvation.

Paul's first address was to the Gentiles among them. Theirs was a society marked by immorality and idolatry, but despite their ignorance about God's law, Paul didn't excuse their behavior.

**Review 1:19–20.**

3. Pop quiz: Which group of people did Paul discuss/address first? (Note: We'll continue to add to this list as we move through these sections, so keep this in mind!)

★ 4. According to 1:20, why are the Gentiles "without excuse"?

In addition to God's revealing Himself generally through His magnificent creation, He also gave all humans—His image-bearers—an embedded moral code, a conscience. Theologians call this *general revelation*.

**Review 1:21–23.**

Even though the Gentiles had a general revelation of God, they exchanged the glorious Creator for a fallen and fleeting creation. They preferred the things of the world to the things of God.

5. How does 1:21–23 describe our society today? Give an example.

**Review 1:24–28.**

At the beginning of the next three paragraphs in this section, Paul used a transition word or phrase. Paul had already told the Roman Christians what the unrepentant Gentiles were guilty of. As he concluded this section, he told them what God did.

★ 6. Complete the table below with Paul's transition phrases and God's responses to the unrepentant Gentiles.

| Verse | What the Unrepentant Gentiles Did | Transition | What God Did |
|---|---|---|---|
| 1:24 | | Therefore | |
| 1:26 | Worshiped and served the creature instead of the Creator | | |
| 1:28 | | | |

**Review 1:29–32.**

When God gave the unbelieving Gentiles over to their sin, His wrath was a *passive* wrath, meaning He didn't give them the gift of repentance, but allowed them to continue in their unnatural ways, working against His holy plan for the world He created. And they got the consequences they deserved.

Because of our God-given consciences, the Ten Commandments are moral laws that make sense. Regardless of their belief or unbelief in Christ, people agree that murder is wrong.

7. Five of the commandments are listed below. Beside each one, write the sins described in 1:24–31 that contradict that commandment.

| | |
|---|---|
| **Honor your father and your mother.** | |
| **You shall not commit adultery.** | |
| **You shall not steal.** | |
| **You shall not bear false witness against your neighbor.** | |
| **You shall not covet ... anything that is your neighbor's.** | |

In case it's tempting to point fingers at the recipients of God's wrath, let's remember that His wrath is what we deserve too.

8. Review the list of the unbelieving Gentiles' sins in 1:29–31. Do you recognize your own sin anywhere in this list?

As we've talked about, all Christians are saints who have already been justified by the righteousness of God through His Son *and* who are being sanctified by the Spirit. But on this side of eternity, we do still sin against God (and more often than we realize). We are saints and we are sinners simultaneously. And as we move forward in our journey of sanctification, we are called to continually confess our sin, agreeing with God that we haven't done as He's instructed us to do.

9. Write a prayer of confession below, agreeing with God about your sin.

# Romans 2:1–11

## † READ ROMANS 2:1-11

When you read about God's wrath and our sin, you may tend toward anxiety, worrying, *Will I experience God's wrath?* Or you may tend toward arrogance, thinking, *Well, that person definitely deserves God's wrath, but not me!* When we fail to have a right view of ourselves, we may find ourselves judging others.

**Review 2:1–2.**

Continuing the discourse he began yesterday, Paul moved on to address a different group of people with a different problem. With each new group, he proved that all have sinned and that all are in equal need of salvation. Again in this section, he followed a similar pattern: This group *"knows who God is, but hasn't responded appropriately to that knowledge, continuing in their sin, and are therefore deserving of God's wrath."*

1. Referencing the ESV, complete the flowchart below with the transition word Paul used to begin this new section. Then use the first sentence of 2:1 to write Paul's opening words to the new group of people.

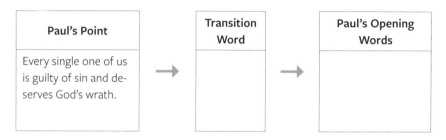

| Paul's Point | | Transition Word | | Paul's Opening Words |
|---|---|---|---|---|
| Every single one of us is guilty of sin and deserves God's wrath. | → | | → | |

Paul addressed the judging Gentile or Jew in this category; we'll refer to them as *moralizers*.

2. Pop quiz: Who were the first two specific groups of the four that Paul addressed?

**Review 2:3.**

There's an interesting shift in Paul's tone here that continues throughout the rest of Romans. It's as if he was having a persuasive conversation with his audience, anticipating questions they'd ask and addressing them. It was a commonly used style of rhetoric in ancient Greco-Roman literature, but it also leads us to wonder if these were real questions he'd been asked throughout his missionary journeys. Be on the lookout for this asked-and-answered writing style throughout the rest of this letter.

★ 3. What's the problem with the moralizers' judgment, according to 2:3? Who is the true Judge?

**Review 2:4–5.**

Moralizers condemn others, and they also attempt to excuse themselves from accountability. They try to manipulate God's character to escape His righteous judgment, thinking, *Because I'm much better than those people, and because God is kind and gracious, I'll avoid God's wrath.*

God *is* kind and gracious, and He's also just. Because He's just, He must judge all sin. And because He's kind and gracious, He leads us to repentance *and* to Himself.

4. According to 2:5, what will happen to the moralizer who tries to manipulate God's character for their own protection?

**Review 2:6.**

In the middle of Paul's explanation of this group's sinful nature and need for a Savior, this verse might sound like a contradiction, but let's remind ourselves of the context.

5. Pop quiz: What group of people was Paul talking about in this section?

Paul wrote about people who thought they were nailing it—they followed the law and publicly performed good works. Like moralizers today, they could probably rattle off a list of their good works, and even produce witnesses, thinking it proved their righteousness. But God is the judge, and He knows the heart behind the works done in public and in private.

**Review 2:7–10.**

★ 6. According to 2:7, what did the recipients of eternal life seek in doing good?

★ 7. According to 2:8, what did the recipients of wrath and fury seek in pretending to do good?

No one is saved because of their own good works, but true salvation will demonstrate itself through rightly motivated good works.

**Review 2:11.**

Before Paul moved on to discuss the next group of people, he reminded his audience that the same fate awaited both unrepentant Gentiles and unbelieving Jews. Gentiles would be held accountable to the general revelation of God. Jews would be held accountable to the special revelation of God—through the Law, the Prophets, and Jesus (more on this tomorrow). But both would be held accountable, and God would be the judge.

# Romans 2:12–29

## ✝ READ ROMANS 2:12-29

Paul, having already proved that unbelieving Gentiles were sinners deserving of God's wrath, wrapped up his discussion of moralizers in today's text.

1. In your own words, define *moralizer*.

**Review 2:12–13.**

Since Paul was talking about both Gentile and Jewish moralizers, he paused to address the law. Remember, Gentiles were mostly ignorant of God's law, but Jews weren't.

Let's take a moment to discuss the three types of laws in Scripture: civil, ceremonial, and moral. **Civil laws** governed the nation-state of Israel and addressed behavior that would protect their nation-state from harm. Many of the **ceremonial laws** related to Israel's interactions with the temple; they gave instructions for worship, sacrifices, and cleanliness. And **moral laws** explained the bare minimum of right and wrong; these laws reveal God's heart—what He is like and what He values.

Today, the Old Testament **civil laws** no longer apply, because God's people are no longer part of a nation-state; Christians live all over the world, in many nations. And the **ceremonial laws** were fulfilled on our behalf by the perfect, ultimate sacrifice of Jesus—so we no longer need to perform sacrifices and purification rituals. And when the Holy Spirit came to indwell believers, we became the temple where God dwells (as opposed to the temple that was in Jerusalem until its destruction in AD 70). As for the **moral laws**, they still stand, because God and His heart remain unchanged.

This understanding of the law will be important in our study of Romans, so let's pause to make sure we've got it. Pop quiz time!

★ 2. What are the three types of law? Briefly explain each type in your own words.

Since the moral law still applies—not for our salvation, but for our good—theologians have a helpful tool for explaining three purposes of the law: as a curb, a mirror, and a guide. First, the law *curbs* violent outbursts of sin and protects safety and societal order. Second, the law *mirrors* who we are back to us, accusing us and showing us our sin. And third, the law is our *guide*, showing what we should and shouldn't do to live a life that pleases God.[1]

We're going to keep revisiting this idea as we study Romans, so it's important that we internalize it. Let's quiz ourselves again.

3. What are three uses of the law? Draw a picture illustrating each use below, then briefly explain each use in your own words.

| A Curb | A Mirror | A Guide |
|---|---|---|
| | | |
| Example: This controls outbursts and keeps order | | |

**Review 2:14–16.**

Paul closed his section on the moralizers by reminding his audience that Gentiles weren't off the hook. Even though the Gentiles were never bound by the Mosaic law, they had a general revelation of God through creation and their consciences: "The work of the law is written on their hearts" (2:15). On judgment day, things done in secret will be made known. For unrepentant sinners, this should be alarming. But for redeemed saints, this is reassuring. God is our judge. He sees and He knows.

**Review 2:17–24.**

Continuing to prove that all have sinned and are in equal need of salvation, Paul moved on to address a new group of people: self-righteous Jews. He followed the same pattern, explaining that they *"know who God is, but haven't responded appropriately to that knowledge, continuing in their sin, and are therefore deserving of God's wrath."*

Just like Paul wasn't talking about *all* Gentiles in 1:18–32, he wasn't talking about *all* Jews here. Remember that Paul, like Jesus, was a Jew. And Paul was also a Christian, urging his fellow Jews—with their shared history and heritage—to have faith in Jesus, their promised Messiah.

Like the Gentiles, Jews also had a general revelation of God. But unlike the Gentiles, the Jews—God's chosen people—were given a special revelation of God. God gave them the Old Testament Scriptures, and from their lineage, He gave them Jesus. But Paul said that despite all of that, some of his fellow

Jews who claimed to love God's law actually ignored it. They failed to practice what they preached, and therefore dishonored—and even blasphemed—God.

4. In 2:21–23, what examples did Paul give of the self-righteous Jews dishonoring God and His law?

| You teach others | | you do not teach yourself |
|---|---|---|
| You preach against stealing | | |
| You denounce adultery | ... but ... | |
| You hate idols | | |
| You boast in the law | | |

**Review 2:25–29.**

When God made a covenant with Abraham, circumcision became a symbol of the covenant, but it wasn't the covenant itself. And when God gave the law, circumcision was required by the law, but it wasn't the entire law. Paul explained that the ritual of circumcision itself didn't save the Jews. (He circles back to this idea in 4:9–12, so we'll revisit it soon.) Essentially, Paul's message was this: *If you're breaking any of God's laws, you may as well be uncircumcised.* And because none of us are capable of fully keeping God's law, circumcision doesn't grant us any additional favor before God.

★ 5. In 2:28–29, what did Paul say a Jew is? Is not? Complete the graphic below. **(If you're stuck, looking at the text in various Bible translations may help you.)**

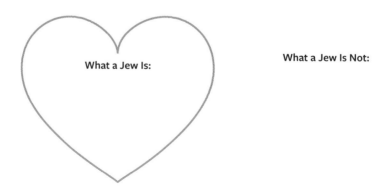

What a Jew Is:

What a Jew Is Not:

We started studying the bad news on Day 2, and we're still studying it. But even in the middle of the bad news, there is good news for the believer. None of us has ever kept the law perfectly, but Jesus did. We all deserve God's wrath, but Jesus bore it for us. We're all in need of a Savior, and our Savior came! He kept the law, He bore the wrath, He made a way to the Father, and He's where the joy is!

6. What stood out to you most in this week's study? Why?

7. What did you learn or relearn about God and His character this week?

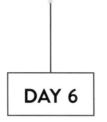

## DAY 6

# Corresponding Psalm & Prayer

 **READ PSALM 106**

1. What correlation do you see between Psalm 106 and this week's study?




2. What portions of this psalm stand out to you most?




3. Close by praying this prayer aloud:

*Father,*
   *Blessed are You, the Lord, the God of Israel! You gather us from*
*among all the nations, and we give You all the thanks, praise, and*

*glory. Even when we've forgotten Your faithfulness, You've been faithful. Even when we've wandered, You've been steadfast. Even when we've sinned, You have forgiven us.*

*Through Your Son's sacrifice, You have made me a saint. And yet until He returns, I'm still a sinner living in this body of flesh. I have been aware of Your law and have chosen to ignore it. I've tried to justify my own sin by comparing it to the sins of others. I've been both an outward sinner and an inward moralizer. I agree with You about my sin—my sins have earned Your wrath—and because I recognize the weight of my sin, I'm so much more grateful for Your forgiveness. Thank You for forgiving me. Thank You for granting me the righteousness of Your Son, Jesus!*

*Remind me that I'm justified because of Jesus. Remind me that I'm being sanctified by the work of Your Spirit, to live and look more like Your Son. I surrender my life to You, Lord—every moment of my day, each decision I make, I yield my will and way to Your perfect will and way.*

*I love You too. Amen.*

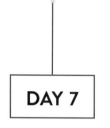

**DAY 7**

# Rest, Catch Up, or Dig Deeper

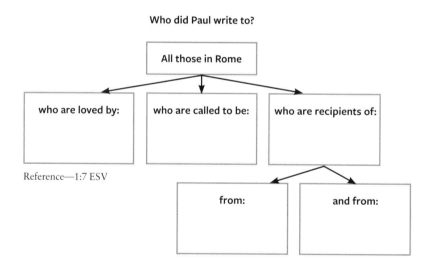

WEEKLY CHALLENGE

Even through trials, Paul's Christian life was marked by his faithfulness. But in his letter, he didn't introduce himself to the Romans with his résumé of good works. He defined himself by Christ. Write an introduction of yourself based on Christ. If it helps, use the diagram to get started.

**Who did Paul write to?**

All those in Rome

who are loved by:

who are called to be:

who are recipients of:

from:

and from:

Reference—1:7 ESV

┌─ Scripture to Memorize ─┐

For the law of the Spirit
of life has set you free
in Christ Jesus from the
law of sin and death.

Romans 8:2

# Romans 3–4

## DAILY BIBLE READING

Day 1: Romans 3:1–8
Day 2: Romans 3:9–20
Day 3: Romans 3:21–31
Day 4: Romans 4:1–12
Day 5: Romans 4:13–25
Day 6: Psalm 32
Day 7: Catch-Up Day

Corresponds to Days 341 and 342 of *The Bible Recap*.

## WEEKLY CHALLENGE

See page 68 for more information.

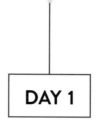

# Romans 3:1–8

 **READ ROMANS 3:1-8**

Earlier, Paul proved that both the unbelieving Gentiles and unrepentant moralizers were sinners deserving of God's wrath. Yesterday he began his address to the self-righteous Jews, and today he concluded his discussion of that third group.

He had just reminded the Jews that simply being a Jew is not what brings righteousness. They claimed membership in the family of God via their ethnicity, heritage, and ability to keep the law. But Paul had just demolished that notion in 2:17–29, so he knew his Jewish brothers and sisters would have questions. He opened this chapter by anticipating two of their questions, then offering the answers.

1. Pop quiz: Who were the first three specific groups Paul addressed?

**Review 3:1–2.**

2. What specific advantage did Paul point out?

When he shared this distinction between Jews and Gentiles, Paul said, "To begin with," causing us to think he was going to offer up a list of the advantages of being a Jew. After all, he did just take significant real estate to bring their high view of themselves down a notch or two. But this phrase "to begin with" actually means "chiefly" or "first" or "most importantly." Paul was pointing out that this advantage was not to be taken for granted; it was a big deal!

**3. In a Greek lexicon or Bible dictionary, look up the word *oracles* (3:2) and list other synonyms.**

Later in his letter, Paul does list other advantages of this heritage—but none of them compares to having heard the actual voice of God.

Paul used an important word in speaking of these oracles. He didn't say they were simply *given* the oracles. He didn't say they were *told* the oracles. He said the Jews were *entrusted with* the oracles of God.

**4. What comes to mind when you think of being entrusted with something versus simply being handed something?**

God could have entrusted His words, instructions, and laws to anyone. But He entrusted them to the Jews. As the popular saying goes, with great power comes great responsibility. Though being entrusted with the oracles of God was an advantage, this was nothing to boast about. When you've heard the clear voice of God, you're held accountable to obey.

**Review 3:3–4.**

God is not like us. Our character is not a benchmark for His character. The Jews may have been full of self-righteousness, but despite their greatest attempts to attain true righteousness, they weren't perfect. Thankfully, their unfaithfulness did not and could not nullify God's faithfulness. When we forget the truth of His faithfulness, our sin can cause great anxiety and distress.

In 3:4, Paul used a phrase we'll see throughout the book of Romans. The phrase "By no means!"—*me ginomai* in Greek—is Paul's adamant, fist-pounding-the-table, look-you-dead-in-the-eye way of saying, "This will *never* be!"

★ 5. Does it comfort you to know God is faithful even when you have failed? How so? Write down a few ways you're grateful that He is not like us. Be as specific as you can. Then praise Him for it!

**Review 3:5–8.**

Paul could hear the peanut gallery even as he was writing. He knew inquiries were coming and headed them off at the pass with more rhetorical questions.

Bear in mind that his initial audience for this letter was the Roman church. So "us" and "we" certainly included Paul and the Romans. And today, as members of the church interacting with a divinely inspired letter that God saw fit to include in His Word, there are many cases where we can also consider ourselves included in the "us" and "we" because Paul was often addressing core principles of our faith.

It's true—our unrighteousness only magnifies God's righteousness, faithfulness, and grace. But that doesn't mean our unrighteousness can be excused by God. This truth led to another possible assumption by Paul's readers: God is unrighteous and selfish for punishing our unrighteousness.

So Paul punched his point with another *me ginomai*—"by no means!" God is God. We are not. That we don't understand His ways is no basis for claiming that His character is flawed. Paul again used his adamant, fist-pounding-the-table, look-you-dead-in-the-eye way of saying, "God is righteous!"

But He *is* holy. God is love—yes—*and* He hates sin. Sin harms us, dishonors Him, and so easily ensnares us (Hebrews 12:1). Because God loves the world, He *must* justly judge our sin.

As for the final rhetorical question of today's reading, Paul didn't even justify it with a retort.

6. What does it reveal about our hearts if we justify sin on the basis of God's faithfulness?

Should we think that the more we sin, the better God looks? *Me ginomai*. May it never be.

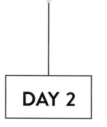

# Romans 3:9–20

## ✝ READ ROMANS 3:9–20

In this section, Paul concluded his chapters-long point by addressing a fourth and final group of people: every single person in the entire human race. Following the same pattern, he explained that they *"know who God is, but haven't responded appropriately to that knowledge, continuing in their sin, and are therefore deserving of God's wrath."* He indicted all of humanity on a single charge: There is none righteous. No, not even one.

1. Pop quiz: Who were the four groups Paul addressed, beginning in 1:18?

**Review 3:9.**

Paul worked hard to paint a clear picture of who this state of unrighteousness applied to.

2. Reiterating Paul's previous point, who is under sin?

Though the Jews received the oracles of God, that didn't give them any advantage toward righteousness. There wasn't something inherently righteous about them. And in fact, there *was* something inherently evil about them—and us. Until Christ redeems us, we are all under sin—"under" meaning: oppressed by it, under its power, ruled by it.

Knowing the Jews in his audience would resist this idea, Paul used the oracles of God to prove his point. He employed six Old Testament passages to tell his audience the truth about the condition of their hearts.

**Review 3:10–18.**

3. Draw a line to connect Paul's quote to its Old Testament reference.

| | |
|---|---|
| Romans 3:10–12 | Isaiah 59:7 |
| Romans 3:13 | Psalm 10:7 |
| Romans 3:14 | Psalm 5:9, Psalm 140:3 |
| Romans 3:15–17 | Psalm 36:1 |
| Romans 3:18 | Psalm 14:1–3 |

4. The Old Testament writers used a series of metaphors to describe sin. How have you seen each of these in a present-day example?

| Metaphor | Examples |
|---|---|
| Throat is an open grave | |
| Venom of asps under their lips | |
| Mouth full of curses and bitterness | |
| Feet are swift to shed blood | |

The Jews, and even the God-fearing Gentiles, might have taken issue with the last line of 3:11, "no one seeks for God." If ever there were a people zealous for God, it was the Jews. They would argue that no one sought after God as vigorously as they did. But even in their seeking, they had evil motives.

★ 5. How can our desire to achieve righteousness through our actions be motivated by evil? Do you ever struggle with this? Briefly describe your struggle.

The most important wake-up call appears in 3:18, "There is no fear of God before their eyes." Humanity's disobedience and stubbornness through the ages testified to the true condition of man's heart apart from Christ.

As the beginning of Paul's list showed, we are *passively* evil—meaning, since the fall of Adam, that is simply who we are. It is our fallen human nature. But notice how 3:13–18 also revealed how *actively* evil we are. We aren't simply wicked people by default; we're active participants in wickedness.

6. Using the diagram below, write the verse numbers next to the parts of the body that participate in unrighteousness.

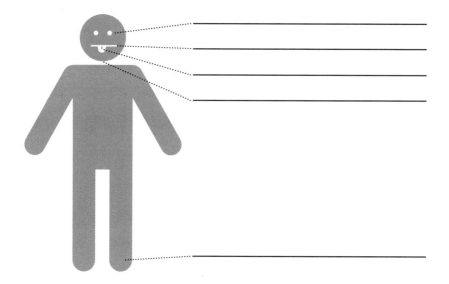

**Review 3:19–20.**

Paul used these Old Testament passages to show the true human condition. As Warren Wiersbe said, these verses present a spiritual X-ray of the lost sinner: We are sinful head to foot.[1]

But what good is an X-ray if there is no treatment to reverse the diagnosis? This is where the law falls short. Paul's point was that the law is useful for a diagnosis, which is crucial. But both the law and our striving for moralism are useless for actual healing.

★ 7. When have you tried to "heal" yourself through religious practices or by striving to "do better"? What was the result?

Thankfully, Paul's audience wasn't left with mere knowledge of sin. The point of his message wasn't to leave them feeling condemned. But he did want them to know the bad news so that they might feel the weight of how sinful they truly were, because that bad news was the beginning of a beautiful story. Tomorrow, we have an opportunity to experience how good the good news is.

# Romans 3:21–31

 **READ ROMANS 3:21-31**

Returning to our spiritual X-ray illustration, the diagnosis was grim. Paul's message in 3:10–20 was clear. He described fallen humanity as not only broken, but terribly wicked too—and the law was a miserable substitute for righteousness. Here, Paul moved into how healing happens and where it comes from.

**Review 3:21–22.**

Right away, Paul mentioned three doctrinal pillars.

1. Fill in the blanks of the following pillars.

　　Righteousness of \_\_\_\_\_

　　The \_\_\_\_\_ and the Prophets

　　_____ in Jesus Christ.

Each of these concepts was crucial to Paul's audience as they sought how to attain favor with God—a struggle not so different from ours.

2. Review Week 1, Day 2's discussion of Romans 1:17. What does *righteousness* mean?

Said another way, "righteousness of God" meant God's requirement for right standing with Him. God does not excuse sin, but He has provided a way to be released from its condemnation. Mirroring his statement in 1:17, Paul essentially said in 3:21–22, *"There's a way of righteousness outside of keeping the letter of the law, and it's through God Himself!"*

But he was quick to say this does not nullify the law; in fact, the Mosaic law and the prophets even testified that this way of release would come.

3. According to 3:21–22, how was the righteousness of God granted to them?

Do not miss the magnitude of this truth. This was—and is—a game-changer for all those who seek to be righteous! It lifts an incredible weight off the shoulders of all who grasp it. When Martin Luther's eyes were opened to the meaning of this passage, he recorded his revelation: "This passage of Paul became to me a gateway to heaven."[1]

**Review 3:23–26.**

Paul introduced three crucial principles for understanding this righteousness apart from the law.

4. **Using a Bible dictionary, define each of the terms in the table.**

| Principle | Definition |
|---|---|
| Justification | |
| Redemption | |
| Propitiation (or Atonement) | |

These terms have very different origins, but they paint a beautifully cohesive picture of what happens when we put our faith in Jesus. **Justification**—a legal term from a courtroom setting—conveys the idea that our record is expunged and our rap sheet is cleared. **Redemption** describes what it takes to set someone free from slavery. **Propitiation** (or atonement) was a religious term used by both Jews and Greeks, and both would've understood the sacrifice it took to "appease" God.

The truth of 3:23 may be familiar to you—it's one of the first verses many learn when hearing the good news of Jesus. But we miss the full beauty of the passage if it's detached from 3:24.

5. Use 3:24 to fill in the blanks.

"And are _____ by his _____ as a _____."

Paul knew law-abiding Jews would try to turn this free gift into another level to be achieved. And if we aren't careful, we'll do the same.

★ 6. **Look up Ephesians 2:8–9.** How did Paul describe faith to the church at Ephesus? How does this bring relief when you feel your faith can't measure up?

Despite all our intentions to trust in Christ alone by faith alone, we, like the Jews Paul was speaking to, tend to believe faith is something we have to muster up to achieve salvation. We may shame ourselves for not having enough faith or worry that our faith isn't strong enough. But that's the beauty of it being a gift! It's *all* free. It's *all* grace. It's *all* because of Jesus.

7. How do we receive this gift of salvation? Circle all that apply.

    A. By the righteousness of God

    B. Through our good works

    C. Through faith in Jesus

    D. By trying hard to have faith

    E. Through the blood of Christ

According to 3:25–26, this was God's plan all along. In His forbearance (restraint), He withheld from pouring out His full wrath until the cross. Only God could be both just and justifier—He makes the rules—and He made a way to appease His own wrath through the death and resurrection of Jesus. He is the one we must stand before.

**Review 3:27–31.**

This news leaves no room for boasting. Christ paid the penalty we couldn't possibly pay on our own. Our blood, sweat, and tears accomplish nothing. But the blood of Jesus cries out for us—to justify us, redeem us, and atone for us.

8. What two concepts did Paul repeatedly highlight in these verses?

These terms are repeated because that was the language of Paul's audience. They were holding the tension of what they'd always known to be their way of religious life *and* what they were learning about the character of God.

★ 9. Both the law and faith are important; they just function differently. Returning to our spiritual X-ray illustration, explain how the law and faith in Jesus work together.

One theologian explained it this way: "Only the gospel allows us to recognize and uphold the perfect standards of the law, because we know that the law matters enough to God for it to bring death; but we know that it no longer means *our* death."[2]

# Romans 4:1–12

 **READ ROMANS 4:1-12**

Romans 3 closed with a word about boasting, reminding the Jewish believers that grace leaves no room for arrogance. Paul followed up the thought in today's reading by using two men who were pillars of the Jewish faith to prove this point.

**Review 4:1–3.**

Abraham served as perhaps the strongest Old Testament evidence that simple obedience to God's laws doesn't yield the righteousness God requires. Paul essentially said, *"Abraham—even Abraham!—wasn't justified by his works, so how could you dare to say* your *works justify you?"*

1. Pulling from what you learned yesterday, describe the concept of justification in your own words below.

To answer his rhetorical question, Paul pointed his audience directly to the text: "What does the Scripture say?" This is an important principle to remember. When discussing any theological issue, it's wise to begin with the question "What does the Scripture say?"

**Review 4:4–5.**

Paul quoted Genesis 15:6, Abraham's moment of salvation. It's important to note that this moment happened when Abraham *was still a Gentile*. We'll come back to that in a moment.

Notice that the text said Abraham "believed God" not "believed *in* God." Read Genesis 15:1–6 to get this verse in context.

2. What did Abraham (who was still called Abram at this point in Genesis) believe God would do?

No one would've blamed Abraham for finding God's promise a little unbelievable. But as we'll see tomorrow, he looked at his circumstances and, against all odds, knew God was able.

★ 3. In what ways do you struggle with believing God, despite believing *in* Him?

The word *counted* is translated from the Greek word *logizomai*. It shows up eight times in today's passage alone, and it's a term used to pronounce a status that was not previously there. Abraham had no claim to righteousness before this moment. To count his belief as righteousness was to bestow on him a status he couldn't produce on his own.

**4. In 4:4–5, Paul contrasted works and the gift of grace. What is required to receive this same declaration of righteousness Abraham received, which is available even to the ungodly?**

**Review 4:6–8.**

In 4:6–8, Paul doubled down on Jewish heritage. Abraham was the father of the Jews, and David was the beloved king of the Jews. But let's not forget: David and Abraham also dealt with failures that had lasting and widespread consequences (Genesis 16; 2 Samuel 11). *And still*, they were counted as righteous. Why? Because their righteousness was based on their faith—not their works.

Similar to the Jewish believers, we tend to overcomplicate the goodness of God and His grace. Believe Him who justifies. Believe that He is able to save. Believe that Jesus meant it when He said, "Whoever believes in me will not perish" (John 3:16). The gospel is as simple as that.

**Review 4:9–12.**

Here it's helpful to recall what we learned in 2:25–29 about circumcision—that it was simply a ritual as part of the law, not an act that led to righteousness before God. Paul used the order of events in Abraham's life to add clarity to this important distinction.

5. **Read Genesis 15:6, then read Genesis 17:10.** Which declaration came first?

The blessing of righteousness couldn't possibly apply only to those who were circumcised if Abraham was "counted as righteous" before he was circumcised. Most theologians agree that the covenant of circumcision happened at least fourteen years after this moment in Genesis 15:6.

The covenant of circumcision is what marked those who would become the Jewish people. That means Abraham *was a Gentile* when he was credited with righteousness. This is a shocking and beautiful truth!

6. Write down the three statements in Romans 4:10–11 that confirm Abraham's declaration of righteousness wasn't based on his circumcision.

★ 7. All this was part of God's plan. In fact, 4:11–12 explicitly says there was a purpose for this order of events. In your own words, explain what this purpose was.

Abraham believed God and it was credited to him as righteousness. Full stop. Salvation comes through faith alone. But that belief also prompted him to "walk in the footsteps of the faith."

Abraham's belief was not merely lip service—he believed God to his core. He was circumcised, yes, but not to earn the righteousness of God. Abraham was circumcised because *he was already righteous before God*, and as an example for those who would follow, he wanted to be a man who lived out of the righteousness he'd been granted.

# Romans 4:13–25

**✝ READ ROMANS 4:13–25**

In today's passage, Paul continued discussing Abraham's faith to remind his audience where righteousness is found and to show them how God kept His promises.

**Review 4:13–16.**

1. What promise did God make to Abraham? And how was it given to him?

In Genesis 15, God specifically promised Abraham that he would have an heir. And not only would he have an heir, but he would be the father of many nations (Genesis 17:4; Genesis 18:18). Believing in that promise is what credited Abraham with righteousness, and as we saw yesterday, this set the example for those who would follow in his steps of faith.

★ 2. In 4:16, what did Paul say the promise rested on? How would that have given relief to his readers—and even you?

The promise itself was anchored in faith—not the law, not works, not a life perfectly lived, but simply taking God at His word.

It is not our pitiful adherence to the law that guarantees the promise. That guarantee is because of grace. Stop for a moment and rest in the hope that brings. Think of all the times you've failed and thought you ruined God's plan for your life—that you couldn't possibly be useful to God, that you're the weakest link in His kingdom. Or maybe you think, *All His plans for me will surely collapse under the weight of my sin!*

The answer to all our second-guessing is the grace that abounds to us through Christ. Your works are not the object of your faith—God is. Abraham was declared righteous, not because of his works, but *despite* his works. Grace creates rest for our weary, anxious hearts.

**Review 4:17–21.**

Here, Paul zeroed in on a simple truth that was the very foundation of Abraham's faith—God is able.

3. In 4:17, what things did Paul say were called into existence?

This is a concept theologians refer to as *ex nihilo*, a Latin term that means "from nothing." Abraham, hoping "against hope" (4:18), knew that the same God who was powerful enough to create the universe from nothing—*ex nihilo*—could also deliver on his promise of an heir, *ex nihilo*.

4. Why would Abraham need to draw on God's power to bring something from nothing? What were his and Sarah's circumstances in 4:19?

Paul wasn't exaggerating. When Abraham tried to picture this promise playing out—his elderly, barren wife holding their newborn child—surely there would be some doubt in his mind, right? But Paul was careful to point out that Abraham *never wavered*. And the last part of 4:20 tells us why.

5. What caused Abraham to grow strong in his faith?

Abraham did not give glory to God as a result of his strengthened faith. His faith was strengthened *because* he gave glory to God. Abraham looked around at his circumstances, held them up against what he knew to be true about God, and believed God was able. So before his wrinkled hands ever held the child, he glorified God.

6. **Look up the following verses.** What do they say about God?

Hebrews 7:25

Ephesians 3:20

2 Corinthians 9:8

★ 7. Is there an area where you are discouraged? Do your circumstances look bleak? Are you finding life to be more disappointing than fulfilling? Use the space below to give glory to God—find ways to thank Him, praise His character, and tell Him you love Him too.

As his faith grew, Abraham became "fully convinced" (4:21) that God would bring this promise to pass. And while Abraham wasn't perfect, God counted him to be righteous. Does this mean that every dream we have and every prayer we pray will come to pass the way we imagine? No. But as we'll see later in Paul's letter, God's plan is being worked out for our good.

**Review 4:22–25.**

Abraham's story was written down for all of us. When we believe that God raised Jesus from the dead to deliver us from our sins, the promise of justification is extended to us as well. When we look at our circumstances and our weaknesses and struggle to find joy in a world that seems to only grow darker by the day, we still have everything we need in our relationship with God. We can rest in the grace of Jesus—because He's where the joy is.

8. What stood out to you most in this week's study? Why?

9. What did you learn or relearn about God and His character this week?

DAY 6

# Corresponding Psalm & Prayer

 READ PSALM 32

1. What correlation do you see between Psalm 32 and this week's study?

2. What portions of this psalm stand out to you most?

3. Close by praying this prayer aloud:

*Father,*
    *I rejoice and am glad in You! Paul wrote that believers are justified by the gift of Your grace (Romans 3:24). And David wrote, "Blessed is*

the one . . . whose sin is covered" (Psalm 32:1). My sin is covered and I'm blessed because of the gift of grace You've given me. Thank You!

My sin is forgiven, but it hasn't been eradicated yet. Until You come back, I'm still a sinner. But even when I fail, You're faithful. So I confess my sin to You now and ask for Your forgiveness. I've pretended to live Your way while inwardly clinging to my sin. Or I've acknowledged my sin and tried to heal myself by doing better. Remind me that only You cover sin.

May I never use who You are—loving and forgiving—to justify my sin. Instead, may who You are prompt me to ask for Your forgiveness and remind me to rest in Your love. All my effort—if not led and empowered by Your Spirit—is futile.

I don't want to walk in the way I think will be the most comfortable or the way I think will make me look best. I want to walk in the footsteps of faith. So I surrender my life to You, Lord—every moment of my day, each decision I make, I yield my will and way to Your perfect will and way.

I love You too. Amen.

# Rest, Catch Up, or Dig Deeper

 **WEEKLY CHALLENGE**

In Day 4 (and many other places in this week's study), Paul reminded us that our actions—good or bad—have no bearing on our righteousness. We're counted as righteous because of *Jesus's* works, not ours. It is by grace alone, through faith alone, in Christ alone.

Make two columns on a sheet of paper.

In one column, list the things you're tempted to think will help you "earn points" with God. Where do you put pressure on yourself to perform for God and others?

In the other column, list the areas where you struggle in sin (past or present). What haunts you? What does Satan use to accuse you? What area of the flesh is the toughest to crucify?

After you've made both lists, find a creative way to cover them with the word *GRACE* in all caps. You can use paint, marker, chalk—anything—but make it bold. When you look at your lists of achievements and short-comings, make it so that all you see is *GRACE*.

# Romans 5–6

┌─ **Scripture to Memorize** ─┐

For God has done what
the law, weakened by
the flesh, could not do.
By sending his own Son
in the likeness of sinful
flesh and for sin, he condemned sin in the flesh . . .

Romans 8:3

## DAILY BIBLE READING

Day 1: Romans 5:1–11

Day 2: Romans 5:12–21

Day 3: Romans 6:1–14

Day 4: Romans 6:15–19

Day 5: Romans 6:20–23

Day 6: Psalm 45

Day 7: Catch-Up Day

Corresponds to Day 342 of *The Bible Recap.*

## WEEKLY CHALLENGE

See page 94 for more information.

# DAY 1

# Romans 5:1–11

 **READ ROMANS 5:1–11**

**Review 5:1–5.**

1. According to 5:1–2, what two things do believers have as a result of our justification by faith?

Take note of the word *access*—a word that implies permission or ability to enter. If grace were a big corporate office, we wouldn't enter it by waiting for an assistant to buzz us in or get us a security pass. We have access to grace at every moment. No one stands as a barrier between God and us. We have access by faith—and not just a nebulous, intangible faith, but faith specifically in the finished work of Christ Jesus.

2. In 5:2–3, what two things did Paul say to rejoice in? What is your immediate reaction to this?

Roman believers were suffering through very real persecution from Rome in the form of exile, execution, and excruciatingly grotesque torture. But in 5:3–5, Paul unpacked an astoundingly powerful and countercultural truth about suffering: Suffering produces hope. *Produces* is not a weak or passive word. And he didn't say hope is a by-product of suffering; he said it's what it produces. This is a cause-and-effect scenario.

★ 3. Do you know anyone who has grown in their faith as a result of suffering? Or how have you seen suffering produce hope in your own life?

It's easy to grasp this concept intellectually, but it can be hard to live out when suffering comes. Or maybe painful experiences from the past feel like a barrier to this belief. It's important to note what Paul was pointing to when he mentioned hope. He wasn't saying that God will always do what we expect or long for Him to do simply because we're His kids and He loves us.

In moments of grief and suffering, our hope is not in a specific earthly result. God deeply cares about every detail of our lives, but His ways and plans are beyond us (Isaiah 55:8–9). God's goodness and faithfulness are not dependent on what does or doesn't happen in our earthly circumstances. His character is proven by what has already happened: the work on the cross that justified us by faith and grants us access into this grace in which we stand.

In 5:5, Paul mentioned hope not putting us to shame. Hope can be a vulnerable feeling amid suffering. After experiencing trials, we can be inclined to expect more trials to follow. We may wonder, *Has God forgotten me? Will He ever come through, or will things keep getting worse?*

★ 4. Was there a time when you feared your hope would put you to shame? What was your hope in?

Paul told the Romans it's God's love that protects believers from hope putting us to shame. And that love is not just sprinkled, it's *poured*. God's Word is always reminding us that our relationship with Him is not the result of our own efforts or strength—it's granted out of His generosity.

**Review 5:6–11.**

5. How is God's abundance shown in 5:6?

Jesus didn't die because humanity deserved it, so there's no room for pride or self-righteousness. In 5:6–8, Paul was making this point again to bring peace in the disagreements happening between the Jewish and Gentile believers over upholding the Mosaic law. For any Jewish believers in the church, he basically said, *"You guys were already following the law when Jesus died—and God was saying you were sinners then."*

*"Therefore,"* Paul told the Romans, *"because you did not earn that He died for you, but were justified by His blood, how much more are you protected from the wrath of God?"* *Wrath* can sound harsh to our modern ears. But this was actually incredible news.

6. Circle all the words from 5:9–11.

| | | |
|---|---|---|
| much more | much less | reconciled |
| more than that | rejoice | lament |

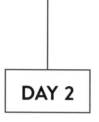

## DAY 2

# Romans 5:12–21

⊕ **READ ROMANS 5:12-21**

1. Review Romans 5:11 from yesterday's reading and fill in the blanks.

"More than that, we also rejoice in God _____ ____ _____ _____

_____, _____ _____ ____ have now _____ _____."

Based on this core truth, today's study takes us through how, in what measure, and why Jesus brought us this reconciliation. There are a lot of steps on the logic journey Paul took his Roman audience through, and we don't want to miss one. His goal in addressing all these details wasn't to be tedious or confusing; on the contrary, he wanted to help his audience gain a thorough understanding of these vital truths.

**Review 5:12–21.**

2. Using 5:12–21, fill in the table below to follow Paul's argument. The first one is filled in for you.

| | |
|---|---|
| sin came into the world | through one man |
| death came | |
| and so death spread to all men because | |
| sin was in the world before | |
| but sin is not counted where | |
| yet death reigned | |
| even over those whose sinning | |
| Adam was a type of | |

Unlike us, Adam began sinless. So Adam was a *type* of "the one who was to come"—Jesus, the only other man to also begin sinless. Adam's sin brought death into the world, and his sin occurred before the law was given. The law—as good as it is—has always been too weak to eradicate sin (Hebrews 10:11).

This is what Paul was referring to by "from Adam to Moses" in 5:14. He wasn't telling the Romans that death reigned *only* from Adam to Moses and then stopped reigning. Moses likely lived during the fourteenth and thirteenth centuries BC. And Paul wrote this letter to the Romans in approximately AD 58. So Paul wasn't forgetting about the time gap between Moses and himself. He was referring to pre-law time. He was (1) explaining how sin entered the world, (2) establishing what was going on with sin in the world prior to the law coming to Moses, and (3) teeing up the good news about the one who was to come, who took care of both sin and the law—defeating sin and fulfilling the law.

★ 3. In your own words, describe what it means that our sin is "not like the transgression of Adam." **Use a commentary or a study Bible for help.**

Jesus is sometimes referred to as the "second Adam"—the new Adam who restored what was destroyed by the first Adam. The world was lost to sin through one man's disobedience, and it was saved by another's obedience. Notice that God doesn't just ask for our obedience; He also modeled it all the way to the cross.

4. **Using a Greek lexicon, look up the one word translated as *free gift* (5:15).** Write the definition or describe it in your own words below.

Paul was explaining that "Adam + Jesus" is not the same thing as "-1 + 1 = 0." When Paul said the free gift wasn't like the trespass, he meant Jesus's free gift of salvation to us is not just equal to the trespass, canceling it out. Instead, it *abounds over* it. The gift is *so much more*.

Everything in the Word of God not only points to God's perfect plan for restoring what was lost by sin, but also brings even more, even better than what was lost. God has an abundance mentality—He's never in need and He always has more than enough—and we see Him reveal it to us throughout Romans. The law came to increase our awareness of our sin, but everywhere we see mentions of His wrath and His judgment, we see His grace, mercy, and love abounding over them.

★ 5. **Using a Greek lexicon, look up the definition and root of** *abounded* **(5:20).** Describe it in your own words below. When you think about your own sin, do you tend to think of God's grace as "abounding"? Why or why not?

Paul ended this passage by acknowledging the huge positional shift salvation brings. Because of Adam, sin reigned, resulting in death for all humanity. Outside of Christ, that end is still death. However, death's reign is superseded by the reign of righteousness through the second Adam—Jesus—who provides life for all who believe. That life is marked by grace that is secure through God's declaration of righteousness.

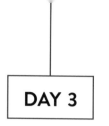

# Romans 6:1–14

## ✟ READ ROMANS 6:1-14

In yesterday's reading, Paul established that where sin increased, grace abounded all the more. In today's passage, he addressed a question that often comes up where grace is introduced: If all our sins are forgiven, why not just keep sinning?

**Review 6:1–2.**

1. How did Paul answer his own question from 6:1? Write 6:2 below in your own words.

**Review 6:3–4.**

In 6:3, Paul reminded the Romans that the answer is displayed in our relationship with Christ through the act and picture of baptism. At this time in history, baptism often involved the use of mikvahs (Jewish ritual baths used for purification) or whatever body of water was available, like a nearby river or lake. Paul knew his audience would picture submersion in water when he mentioned baptism, and he wanted them to connect that visual with a burial, where a body is lowered into the ground.

When we step into a life of grace through faith in Christ, our old ways are buried so that we might walk in newness of life as we're raised up. This newness of life comes with a new heart—one that loves God—and a new Spirit—one that has the power to walk in obedience instead of in sin. We have unity with Him in death so that we might have unity with Him in new life and resurrection.

★ 2. What's the difference between using grace as an excuse to keep sinning and accepting grace as an invitation to a new way of living? Can you see examples of either in your own life? If so, describe.

**Review 6:5–11.**

Paul mentioned dying or being crucified with Christ multiple times in this section of today's reading. And though many Christians in Paul's time *did* die for Christ, and many around the world still do, that's not what Paul was talking about here. He was addressing the power of what happens in the spiritual realm when we follow Christ. This was a continuation of his baptism/burial metaphor: There is no resurrection without a death first.

But the subsequent resurrection is much greater than the death that preceded it. Once again, Paul was explaining God's generous spiritual math. He bids us come and die—*so that we might live.* Jesus said, "I came that they may have life and have it abundantly" (John 10:10).

3. On the left side of the cross below, write what is put to death in 6:5–8. On the right side, write what comes on the other side of that death. The first one has been filled out for you.

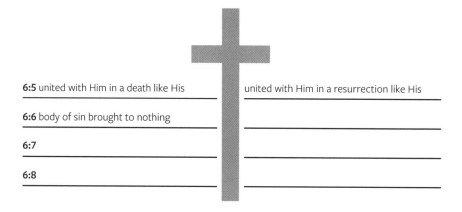

**6:5** united with Him in a death like His

united with Him in a resurrection like His

**6:6** body of sin brought to nothing

**6:7**

**6:8**

With this concept of putting sin to death, the question arises, Then why do we still sin?

4. Yesterday's study ended with 5:21. What key word in that verse appears twice?

That word implies kingly rule, a throne—and it's a helpful idea for understanding the distinction here. In the old self, sin was on the throne. In the new self, which is united with Christ, Christ is on the throne. Sin is still a present enemy seeking to destroy us—it is actively opportunistic—but by Christ's power, we now have authority over it. We're dead to its reigning power forever.

5. What words and phrases in 6:9–10 declare the finished work of Christ?

Paul also reminded the Romans, and even us today, that this life is not about personal freedom. When we're living in a posture of self-focus, thinking, *What can I get away with and still have God forgive me?*, we're forfeiting a life of joy and usefulness for His kingdom.

**Review 6:12–14.**

★ 6. What did Paul call their members in 6:13?

    A. Useful body parts

    B. Mere skin and blood

    C. Instruments for righteousness

    D. Tools for wickedness that must be punished

In Christ, believers are invited into a life where our bodies are used for His glory, instead of being ruled by fleshly desires for comfort and pleasure. "Instruments" could be better translated as weapons or tools of a trade—like a doctor's instrument. But a musical instrument might make the same powerful point. Our lives will produce music of some kind. In this new life of freedom and joy, let it be worship.

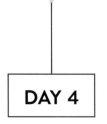

# DAY 4

# Romans 6:15–19

 **READ ROMANS 6:15–19**

Today's passage began with a question that may feel familiar. In 6:1, Paul asked the Romans the rhetorical question "What shall we say then? Are we to continue in sin that grace may abound?"

**Review 6:15.**

1. What did Paul ask in 6:15 that is similar to 6:1?

Paul wasn't repeating himself or circling back to what he'd already said. He was making a slightly different, nuanced point about sin. The verb tense in 6:1 indicated habitual sin, but in 6:15, the verb tense indicated something more like "every now and then."

In addressing occasional sins, Paul wasn't implying that it's possible to cease sinning altogether. He was breaking down the truth about sin: how it operates, how it drives us, and where we find freedom from it. This is why he chose slavery as his example in 6:16–19. He said, "You are slaves of the one whom you obey."

**Review 6:16–18.**

★ 2. Identify the desires you tend to obey that lead to sin. Think beyond the surface desire (greed, lust, vanity, etc.) to the deeper desire beneath it. These may be things you're aware of in the moment, or they may be things you don't realize until later were driving your actions. Briefly describe what you discover.

Our appetites can reveal our true intentions. Maybe you made a sexual decision not out of lust, but out of a craving for affirmation or acceptance. Maybe you were dishonest not out of malice, but out of fear of man or the desire to control others. There are always appetites and cravings driving our intentions to sin, and Paul was telling the Romans to be aware of that. Grace is not about freedom to sin; it's about the marvelous freedom *from* sin and all the bondage that comes with sin. When we become more aware of what's motivating our sin, we can walk in the Spirit's greater power over it.

3. **Read James 4:1–4 in the NKJV.** Where do wars and fights come from?

Paul spent much of this letter to the Romans mapping out the intellectual reasoning for all this gospel truth. But in 6:17, he referred to obedience that comes from the heart—not a begrudging obedience, but a true desire to obey and glorify God. He thanked God that they had become "slaves of righteousness."

Perhaps that phrase makes you smile if you've tasted the bondage of sin and know the freedom of Christ. But perhaps you find yourself uncomfortable with the word *slave*. Perhaps you don't think of yourself as a slave to anything. Paul was telling the Romans everyone serves *something*. It's more obvious in some cases than others, such as addiction, workaholic behavior, and habitual rage. But God's Word says we all have the tendency to let desires drive us.

4. Write a prayer asking God to reveal any places where desires, maybe even for very good things, have led you to obey them instead of God.

God is the giver of every good and perfect gift (James 1:17), and really believing this truth can free us to live in obedience from the heart. The more we trust God as "slaves of righteousness," the more we rest in obedience, trusting that His ways are better and that they work in accordance with His plan for those who love Him (as we'll learn in Romans 8). That was true for Paul's Roman readers, and it's equally true for us who are in Christ.

**Review 6:19.**

In 6:19, Paul apologized for using slavery as a metaphor. Many in his Roman audience were slaves, but he knew it was an effective means of articulating the point *because* of their relationship with slavery and its pervasiveness in the culture. He knew it, like any good metaphor, would help them put a name to something that had previously been unnamed. He was helping them see the way sin can masquerade as freedom to choose when in fact it's merely slavery to a lesser master.

5. What do you think "lawlessness leading to more lawlessness" means?

Seventeenth-century British scholar Thomas Fuller said about sin: "Let us stop the progress of sin in our soul at the first stage, for the farther it goes, the faster it will increase."[1]

★ 6. Can you think of a time when you ended up in a sin spiral or snowball where one sinful choice led to another sinful choice? Do you remember feeling caught in it, like you had no way out? Describe.

Paul told the Romans the way out: becoming "slaves to righteousness."

7. One of God's names is *Jehovah Tsidkenu*. **Look it up in a Bible dictionary.** What does it mean?

# Romans 6:20–23

 READ ROMANS 6:20–23

Throughout Romans 6, Paul has discussed the ways grace frees us not *to* sin but *from* sin. Today, he wrapped it up with a bit of a "gotcha" moment.

**Review 6:20–22.**

1. What do you think Paul meant when he said, "You were free in regard to righteousness"?

He was laying out yet another equation: Being slaves of one thing makes us free from the other thing. When we're slaves of Christ, we're free of the weight of sin. But when we're slaves of sin, we're free of the benefits of Christ, such as righteousness.

2. Summarize Paul's poignant question in 6:21 in your own words.

It's easy to be lured into thinking sinning gets us what we want. Theft can quickly get you money or possessions, but what you gain won't last. Satisfying a desire of the flesh can bring temporary relief, but Paul asked his Roman readers to consider what actual benefit they got from it. In addition to the shame sin brings, he compelled them to look at their lives *after* the sin occurred. If sin was a seed, what fruit did it produce?

★ 3. Where have you previously planted a seed of sin that bears bad fruit now—fruit that may bring feelings of shame?

God tells us no one who hopes in Him will ever be put to shame (Psalm 25:1–3). Paul's goal wasn't to inflict shame on his audience; his goal was to point out that if they already felt shame, it was the natural result of sin. He was encouraging the Romans not to be naive about sin's impact so that they might be more motivated not to sin in the future.

Yesterday we discussed the idea of "lawlessness leading to more lawlessness" (6:19). Paul continued that discussion here and illustrated it with a metaphor of seeds and fruit. A single acorn, over time, has the genetic ability to populate the entire world with trees. The nature of seeds is that their impact is exponential. From one seed, many plants in many areas can eventually grow.

★ 4. Can you think of an area in your life where you've been set free from sin and now have the joy of seeing good fruit where there used to be bad fruit? If so, describe.

5. What does Paul say about the fruit we get as slaves of God (6:22)?

    A. It is delicious but unfulfilling.

    B. It is a prickly pear.

    C. It's bitter to the taste but it nourishes us.

    D. It leads to sanctification and its end, eternal life.

The end of sin's fruit is death. But the end of the fruit we get as slaves of God is eternal life. Here, "end" (6:22) is best translated as "outcome." But thinking of this word in the context of the end of a story is a great way to comprehend the profound news Paul shared here. Scripture says God set eternity in our hearts (Ecclesiastes 3:11). Inherently, we all long for good endings, for happily ever afters, and that desire is planted in our hearts by God Himself. And the good news is that He has a good ending waiting for us!

Perhaps eternal life sounds intimidating, boring, or hard to fathom. Perhaps you long for an itinerary. But we have to remember who we're dealing with here. Eternal life with God is certain to exceed our desires and expectations!

6. As we discussed yesterday, James 1:17 says every good and perfect gift is from above. What is God called in the second part of that verse?

The God who invented the stars is the God who picks out all He has for you. (We dive deeper into eternal life in the weekly challenge!) Rest assured: Eternal life with God isn't just the preferable alternative to hell. It's the ultimate fulfillment of all the good your heart has ever longed for, and all it didn't even know to long for.

**Review 6:23.**

Paul ended the chapter with a verse you may have heard before as a stand-alone passage on a coffee mug or T-shirt. It's a well-known verse with a mighty gospel truth. But if you're familiar with it, don't let familiarity cause you to miss the details.

7. In 6:23 below, circle the two sets of opposites.

> "For the wages of sin is death, but the free gift of God is eternal life in Christ Jesus our Lord."

*Wages* invokes visions of effort, hard labor, and toil for pennies. But when God's the master of our lives, we're not talking wages. We're talking the *free gift* of freedom and eternal life with Him! And what could be better than eternity with the King of all good things? He's where the joy is!

8. What stood out to you most in this week's study? Why?

9. What did you learn or relearn about God and His character this week?

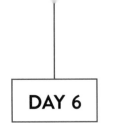

**DAY 6**

# Corresponding Psalm & Prayer

✝ **READ PSALM 45**

1. What correlation do you see between Psalm 45 and this week's study?

2. What portions of this psalm stand out to you most?

3. Close by praying this prayer aloud:

*Father,*
   *My heart overflows with praise for You! You've defeated death and given life. You've forgiven sin and given grace. You sent an eternal*

*King to invite people from all nations to join Your everlasting kingdom. May all the generations remember Your name, and may Your people praise You forever!*

*You're the Reconciler and You've restored me to a right relationship with You. I'm no longer a slave to sin, yet I've kept on sinning. I confess my sins to You now and pray that You will free me from sin's power.*

*You never promised that I wouldn't suffer. May any suffering I endure for Your sake not lead me to sin. Like Paul wrote, may my suffering produce hope.*

*You gave me a body, mind, and spirit that I can use for Your glory. You invite me into the work You're doing. Teach me how to use the gifts You've given me for righteousness. Make me a useful tool for Your kingdom. Make me an instrument of Your praise. I surrender my life to You, Lord—every moment of my day, each decision I make, I yield my will and way to Your perfect will and way.*

*I love You too. Amen.*

# Rest, Catch Up, or Dig Deeper

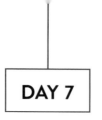 **WEEKLY CHALLENGE**

On Day 5 of this week's study, Paul told the Romans the wonderful news that "the free gift of God is eternal life in Christ Jesus our Lord" (6:23). Write down three to five ideas you have about what "eternal life" entails. Find the scriptural passages that support those beliefs. Make note of any places where you're surprised by what you find.

# Romans 7

## DAILY BIBLE READING

Day 1: Romans 7:1–3

Day 2: Romans 7:4–6

Day 3: Romans 7:7–12

Day 4: Romans 7:13–20

Day 5: Romans 7:21–25

Day 6: Psalm 1

Day 7: Catch-Up Day

Corresponds to Day 342 of *The Bible Recap.*

## WEEKLY CHALLENGE

See page 120 for more information.

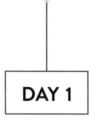

# Romans 7:1–3

## † READ ROMANS 7:1–3

Last week's reading focused on the idea that freedom from the law doesn't mean freedom to sin. Paul knew his audience was well acquainted with the law, so today, we're going to make sure we're on the same page with the author and his initial readers.

**Review 7:1.**

These Romans were believers, so it's fitting that Paul called them "brothers." In a spiritual sense, they were family! As Paul set up his first rhetorical question in Romans 7, he reminded the Romans that despite having never visited them in person, he knew they would've been incredibly familiar with "the law."

1. **Using a Greek lexicon, look up the word used for *law* in 7:1.** What does it mean?

In our English Bibles, we read "the law" (7:1). But in Greek, Paul's words would've read, "I am speaking to those who know law." Scholars disagree as to whether Paul was referring to the Mosaic law or to secular Roman law. Regardless, Paul knew the Romans understood that laws don't apply to dead people. Death ends all contracts and obligations.

2. **Look up the word *law* in an English dictionary.** What does it mean?

Today, laws are rules we live under so we can have an organized and flourishing society. The Mosaic law was given by God to the Israelites to promote a distinct and prosperous way of life. God wanted His people to look different from the rest of the world. If they lived differently, other nations would notice and turn to God.

God gave His people 613 laws in the Torah (the first five books of the Old Testament). And in Romans 7, the word *law* shows up twenty-three times. Regardless of which law Paul was referring to in 7:1, we can be certain the rest of Romans 7 refers to the Mosaic law.

★ 3. **Look up the following passages concerning the Mosaic law, read them carefully, and fill in the table below.**

| Verse | Who was speaking? | Summarize the verse(s) in your own words |
|---|---|---|
| Exodus 19:5–6 | | |
| Leviticus 19:2 | | |
| Leviticus 20:7–8 | | |
| Deuteronomy 30:15–18 | | |

★ 4. Look back at the introduction and list out the three uses of the law below. Then, define them in your own words.

**Review 7:2–3.**

Paul answered his own rhetorical question with an illustration. Everyone would have agreed that if a married woman were living with a man who wasn't her husband, she would be committing adultery. But if her husband died, she would be free to remarry. Paul wasn't necessarily commenting on the biblical guidelines surrounding divorce and remarriage. He was reminding the Romans of the impact death has on the law. Death terminates all laws and contracts.

5. Fill in the blanks in 7:2 below.

"For a married _____ is bound by law to _____ husband while he lives, but if ____ husband dies ____ is released from the law of marriage."

This example would have been abundantly clear to the Romans. Under Jewish law, women weren't allowed to file for divorce. Only men had this ability. A man could find a way out of the marriage contract, but a woman had no power to change her circumstances. For her, death was the only path of release from a marital contract.

Paul made it clear that death had a big impact on contracts. Hold on to the idea of human contracts ending in death, because tomorrow we're going to look at the impact of the one who has defeated death!

6. Write Galatians 3:24–25 in the space below.

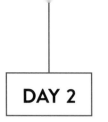

# Romans 7:4–6

 **READ ROMANS 7:4–6**

Paul began today's text with the word *likewise*. This should clue us in that he's about to show the Romans how to personalize the illustration he just presented.

**Review 7:4.**

Death ends all contracts, and Paul explained that as believers, we've died and have been set free from the law. We've died to sin and the law and risen with Christ! This death and resurrection means we've entered into a new relationship with God, one that can yield fruit that's honoring to Him. Apart from Christ, we're powerless to bear *any* fruit.

1. Write Galatians 2:19–20 in the space below.

While we've died to the Mosaic law, we haven't died to the entire Old Testament. Christians today and the Romans Paul was writing to should simply interact with the Old Testament differently. Because we've died with Christ, we're no longer required to live by the civil and ceremonial commands of the law. Praise God! Yet at the same time, the Old Testament is still the authoritative Word of God for our lives (2 Timothy 3:16–17; Hebrews 4:12).

Scholars often present this concept as "the spirit of the law versus the letter of the law." The letter of the law refers to explicit commands including those we're no longer required to follow. The spirit of the law refers to the heart or values of God that are demonstrated through the commands. Those same values and moral principles should still mark believers today.

Now that we have a new relationship with God and the law, our lives can yield fruit. The tricky thing is, this fruit isn't something we can work to manufacture or grow by ourselves. It's something the Spirit creates in us as we yield to His presence in our lives. Fruit typically doesn't grow overnight. It grows over time and relies on forces outside the plant's control (rain, sunlight, soil, etc.) to flourish. Similarly, we rely on the power of the Spirit to produce fruit in our lives as we yield to Him.

Think about it. People who don't know Jesus (who don't have the Holy Spirit) can do morally good things—they can give to charities, obey the speed limit, and let others merge in traffic. God's people, on the other hand, are the only ones who can walk with the Spirit and bear *His* fruit. This is what it means to glorify God (John 15:8).

In Galatians 5, Paul lists works of the flesh and fruit of the Spirit. The works primarily consist of behaviors—things like fits of anger, drunkenness, and sorcery. And these negative choices can be made instantaneously.

In contrast, the fruit is primarily character qualities—things like joy, patience, and kindness. While the works can be chosen in an instant, the fruit (though we could momentarily choose behaviors that look like the fruit) grows stronger over time as the Spirit sanctifies us. We can continue in the works of the flesh through our own choices, but we can only continue producing fruit if the Spirit is at work.

★ 2. Do you ever think you can do things for God or work for Him? In what areas do you tend to rely on your own disciplined efforts rather than on the God who is at work within you to produce His fruit?

**Review 7:5.**

Paul described what life was like before we died with Christ. When we were under the law, we didn't have the Spirit, and sin was just as wrong as it is today. This made us want to sin even more! Paul refers to this period as the time when we were "living in the flesh." The "flesh" is our broken and sinful human nature.

3. **Using a Greek lexicon, look up the word *flesh* (7:5) and write the definition below.**

We're inclined to do the opposite of what God says is best. So the more something is forbidden, the more we'll want to do it. It's kind of like junk food. It tastes great, and the more we eat it or smell it, the more our appetite for it grows. But an increasing amount of junk food in our bodies over time ultimately leads to unhealth, and in some cases, even death.

That's the point Paul's making here. The more we see sin, the more we want it. And the more we want it, the more we partake in it. And the more we partake in it, the faster we're headed toward our demise, as all sin ultimately leads to death.

★ 4. Describe a time when you experienced the human tendency to gravitate toward sin.

**Review 7:6**

Because the Romans had died with Christ, they were no longer under the old way of the "written code" (a.k.a. the Mosaic law); instead, they were able to serve God the new way, through the empowering of His Spirit. One theologian says it's as if "God shifted the transmissions of our lives into neutral gear. Now something else drives our lives, namely, the Holy Spirit."[1]

# Romans 7:7–12

 **READ ROMANS 7:7–12**

After illustrating and personalizing this concept about the law for the Romans, Paul evaluated himself. How did *he* relate to the law?

**Review 7:7.**

The law itself wasn't sin. It merely put labels on sin. Or said differently, it called sin "sin." Think about the importance of labels in a grocery store. How would you know which cans contained pinto beans and which cans contained green beans if they were all unlabeled? The law was like a spiritual label maker. It gave sin names.

1. Which sin did Paul use as an example (7:7)? **Look up its definition in a dictionary and write it below.**

"You shall not covet" is the tenth of the Ten Commandments (Exodus 20:17). It's the only command that targets the intentions or desires of a person's heart rather than tangible actions. The condition of the heart can't be seen, but it can be labeled.

★ 2. What labels would you put on the condition of your heart? What motives or desires have you been wrestling with that God has revealed as sinful? Fill in the labels below.

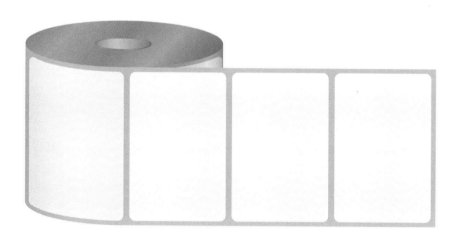

Ultimately, all our actions are rooted in our desires. The law showed Paul (and the Romans) just how broken our hearts and desires are. We're corrupted by sin. Not only did the law label Paul's sin but it also acted like a mirror (as we discussed back in Romans 2). It showed Paul his own sinful nature.

If you look in a mirror and find you've got food stuck in your teeth, you won't like what you see—and the problem isn't with the mirror. The problem is the kale in your incisors.

**Review 7:8.**

The sin in Paul used the law to stir up a desire to disobey God repeatedly. But how did that happen? The law was the track sin longed to run on. Here in 7:8, Paul began to personify sin.

3. What is personification? **Use a dictionary or do a web search for help.** Write the definition below.

★ 4. List the action words Paul used to personify sin.

### Review 7:9–10.

The law promised life in that if all people had always obeyed it perfectly, it would've led to life and flourishing; however, no one could perfectly obey it, so it revealed spiritual deadness (our separation from God).

Paul wrote he was "once alive apart from the law," explaining that before he realized just how spiritually dead he was, he was self-righteous—he didn't recognize his own sinfulness. But when the law labeled his sin, he saw it and he wanted to sin all the more.

Satan loves to take things God meant for good and use them for evil (John 10:10). While God intended for the law to form a stable society (civil laws), regulate man's relationship with God (ceremonial laws), and promote righteous living (moral laws), sin became the active ingredient in Paul's (and everybody else's) relationship with the law.

### Review 7:11

Paul continued personifying sin. It was the active agent in his flesh that pushed him toward evil and away from God's best. If this were a movie, Paul would've been casting his sinful flesh as "the tempter." Paul's sinful nature urged him to do the very things the law prohibited.

When Paul looked in the "mirror" of the law, he saw that not only was he a sinner but he was spiritually dead. Sin doesn't just ruin your life. It makes you lifeless.

**5. Read James 1:14–15 and fill in the flowchart below.**

| | | |
|---|---|---|
| [ ] | → | Temptation |
| Desire when it's conceived | → | [ ] |
| "Fully grown" sin | → | [ ] |

**Review 7:12.**

Because the law comes from God, it must reflect His character. God is holy and good, so the law must be as well. The law, therefore, prescribed what was best for God's people. For example, God's people were forbidden from eating pork (Deuteronomy 14:4–8). Interestingly, swine are distinctively prone to a parasite that can't be seen by the human eye and can never be removed once it enters a human body—and if it enters, it makes people quite sick. And the Israelites didn't have meat thermometers like we do today.

Even when it came down to something as simple as what's for dinner, God intended the very best for His people. As Paul repeatedly told the Romans, the problem wasn't with the commandments their holy God gave them.

The problem lives in us, and it has a name: sin.

## DAY 4

# Romans 7:13–20

### READ ROMANS 7:13-20

Today, we'll explore Paul's struggle with sin. Scholars disagree on whether Paul was referring to his life before or after Christ, but most agree it was the latter. After all, it's uncommon for lost people to care about obeying the commands of a God they don't know and love.

**Review 7:13.**

Through a rhetorical question, Paul made it clear that sin is the only thing that leads to death. It isn't the standard set by the law that makes us dead—it's our sin.

1. Look at yesterday's lesson. What were the two illustrations used to teach us about the law?

The law was like a _____ _____, because it gave sin a name.

The law was like a _____, in that it reflected how sinful we truly are.

Remember how Paul personified sin? Sin is opportunistic. It used the law to grow the desire for sin. It took what God intended for good and twisted it for evil purposes.

**Review 7:14–17.**

Many commentators believe that by calling the law "spiritual," Paul was acknowledging that he didn't have a problem with the law or the good

God who gave it. Instead, he was reminding the Romans that the problem resided in sinful flesh. Paul said he was "sold under sin"—while the law itself was sinless, he himself was sinful. But the law didn't have the power to solve the Romans' (or anyone's) sin problem.

Paul struggled to explain why the problem played out the way it did. He wanted to do what honored God, but instead he did the opposite. He felt this tension within himself. He would disapprove of, yet still do, the very behaviors he knew to be wrong.

★ 2. Have you ever done something you knew was wrong? Maybe you felt deep down you shouldn't do it, but for some reason you felt a seemingly irresistible urge to do it anyway. Explain.

Paul recognized it was good that the things the law labeled as wrong he also thought were wrong. However, it didn't matter how many things the law labeled as sin. He was still going to be inclined to make poor choices.

More laws or rules would never solve the war raging within him. Laws may guide behavior, but they're powerless to change hearts.

It's worth noting that Paul wasn't making excuses for his sin or justifying sinful behavior. In Romans 3, he established that everyone is guilty and without excuse for their sin. He was working to understand *why* he still sinned despite knowing and wanting to do what was right.

3. Look at today's text, then fill in the table below.

| I do not do what I want | I do the very thing I hate |
|---|---|
| If I do what I don't want | |
| | But not the ability to carry it out |
| I don't do the good that I want | |
| | It's the sin that dwells in me |

**Review 7:18–20.**

Paul was tracking down the source of the problem. Though he had died to sin in an eternal sense, his sinful nature was very much alive. He wanted to do what was right and holy, but in his own strength, he couldn't honor God. Paul was a Christian, but like all Christians, he was fallen.

4. When we keep falling back into the same sin, it can be defeating. Paul alluded to this frustration through his use of repetition. How many times did he use the word *want* in 7:13–20?

★ 5. When you want to do what's right but are struggling to fight sin, do you ever let anyone else know about your struggle? Why or why not?

It's encouraging to remember the apostle Paul, who wrote at least thirteen New Testament books, was human like us. Despite finding salvation through faith in Christ's life, death, burial, and resurrection, he still battled sin as a Christian and readily identified himself as both a sinner and a saint.

Sometimes people make the mistake of thinking that once they're saved, they won't struggle with sin anymore; but that's not true. Scripture shows us that even as saved saints, we will still fall short of God's glorious standard in our day-to-day lives. Thanks be to God, we're not alone in that struggle, and our sin doesn't have the final say!

**6. Look up the following verses and write a brief summary in the space below.**

James 5:16

1 Corinthians 10:13

Ecclesiastes 7:20

1 John 1:9

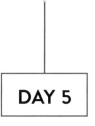

# Romans 7:21–25

READ ROMANS 7:21–25

Today's reading began with the word *so*. This should alert us that Paul was ready to present a conclusion about his desire to do what is good and his inability to follow through.

**Review 7:21.**

When you look up a word in a dictionary, you typically see several definitions listed. When Paul wrote, "I find it to be a law," he was saying something like, *"I find this to be a rule for life on this earth,"* or, *"Believers are universally subject to this principle."* Paul had already used the word *law* repeatedly, and now he's used nearly every variation of it!

★ 1. Draw a line to match each corresponding verse reference and "law" description with its corresponding title.

| | |
|---|---|
| Romans 2:17–18—The law was instruction given by God through Moses to the Jewish people, detailed in the Torah, and, most notably, includes the Ten Commandments. | Law of faith |
| Romans 3:21, 27–28, 4:20–24—This law says entrance into the family of God isn't based on self-righteous acts; rather it's granted through faith in Christ. | Law of God |
| Romans 7:21—The law is a governing truth that marks life on Earth | Law of the mind |
| Romans 7:22—The law refers to God's Word in a general sense. It typically refers to the Torah but can be extended to include the entirety of the Old Testament | Law of Moses |
| Romans 7:23a—The law shows all people are inclined toward and prone to sin while living life in their fallen bodies | Law of the spirit |
| Romans 7:23b—The law proves that while our desires can align with the moral code of the law of Moses, we are powerless to act on these desires because the law of sin is present | Law of sin |
| Romans 8:2—The law proves the Christian who yields to the Spirit's presence within them can be delivered from the law of sin | Law as a principle |

2. Write Genesis 4:7 below.

Even as believers, we still live in the reality that sin is always nearby—it's "crouching at the door." Here, Paul rewound the tape of God's grand rescue plan for humanity all the way back to one of the earliest examples of the law of sin in action: the story of Cain and Abel. Cain yielded to sin, ignored God's instruction, and killed his brother in Genesis 4.

**Review 7:22–23.**

Paul had a genuine appreciation for God's Word. He treasured it. Yet he recognized that, while he loved God's instruction, his sin nature wouldn't go away and it opposed his love for God's Word.

The expression "in my members" was Paul's fancy way of saying there was a war going on inside him. The law of sin (all people are prone to sin) stood in opposition to the law of the mind: As Christians, while we may want to obey God's instruction, we're powerless to do so because the law of sin is binding.

On their own, our desires, thoughts, and even best intentions don't stand a chance against sin.

3. Write Galatians 5:17–18 below. Circle the two opposing sources of desire.

Paul recognized this truth and felt trapped. He couldn't come up with a pathway out of this reality on his own.

★ 4. When you feel frustrated by your own sin, how do you act? What emotions surface in your heart when you encounter a recurring pattern? Explain.

**Review 7:24–25.**

In summary, Paul wrote that he served, or agreed with, the law of God via his thought life (he worked hard to follow the law and desired to obey it) but because of his sinful nature, he still fell short. So who could free Paul (and everybody else) from this frustrating tension? Jesus provided a way of escape!

5. When you find yourself sinning, do you remind yourself there's victory over sin through Christ? If not, what might it look like to regularly remind yourself of this truth?

Read 1 Corinthians 15:2–10 and 15:56–57. Paul made it clear we have victory over sin not because of anything we can do on our own, but because of the finished work of Christ. Thanks to His life, death, resurrection, and ascension, and the work of the Spirit (more on that next week), everything changed. On our own, we were stuck. But because of Christ, we have all the help and hope we need. He's where the joy is!

6. What stood out to you most in this week's study? Why?

7. What did you learn or relearn about God and His character this week?

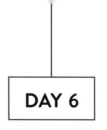

## DAY 6

# Corresponding Psalm & Prayer

 **READ PSALM 1**

1. What correlation do you see between Psalm 1 and this week's study?

2. What portions of this psalm stand out to you most?

3. Close by praying this prayer aloud:

*Father,*
    *I delight in Your law! It reveals who You are. It teaches me what to do and reminds me that I'm Your heir. And as Your heir, I get to*

*be a part of the work You're doing and the story You're writing—what a joy and a blessing!*

*Like a mirror, the law also shows me my sin, which I confess to You now. I've wanted for myself what You have given to others. I've pointed out the sins of others while not even pausing to examine my own. I've been quick to anger, and my anger has not been righteous.*

*Like a label maker, the law also labels my sin. I have coveted. I have been prideful. I have been filled with rage and resentment.*

*Even though "I do the very thing I hate" (Romans 7:15), You deliver me from sin and death. Your Son's death didn't end Your covenant; it opened Your covenant to anyone who would believe, including me. Thank You, Lord!*

*So let me meditate on You and on Your law day and night. May every day be a new chance to praise You and to please You with my thoughts, words, and actions. I surrender my life to You, Lord—every moment of my day, each decision I make, I yield my will and way to Your perfect will and way. I commit to walking in Your way.*

*I love You too. Amen.*

# Rest, Catch Up, or Dig Deeper

 **WEEKLY CHALLENGE**

Though the law revealed Paul's sin, he affirmed its goodness because it came from a holy God. Since we've died with Christ, as we read on Day 2, we're no longer bound by the civil and ceremonial commands of the law. However, the Old Testament remains both beneficial to our lives and formative to our relationship with God. Choose an Old Testament passage (e.g., Psalm 119) and spend twenty minutes meditating on it. Set a timer, eliminate distractions, and open your Bible.

Meditation—as demonstrated in Scripture—is devoting uninterrupted time to focus on God and His Word. Think about the passage's implications. Look for truths about God. Pray through it or even work to commit it to memory. Make note of anything that stands out to you.

# Romans 8

## DAILY BIBLE READING

Day 1: Romans 8:1–11

Day 2: Romans 8:12–17

Day 3: Romans 8:18–25

Day 4: Romans 8:26–30

Day 5: Romans 8:31–39

Day 6: Psalm 44

Day 7: Catch-Up Day

Corresponds to Day 343 of *The Bible Recap.*

## WEEKLY CHALLENGE

See page 144 for more information.

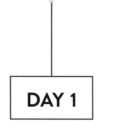

# Romans 8:1–11

 **READ ROMANS 8:1–11**

**Review 8:1–4.**

We've seen Paul use *therefore* to connect sentences and paragraphs, but here he used that simple word to link everything he's said so far in Romans 3–7 to yet another liberating and extraordinary theological truth.

Because of *all* God did through Jesus, there is no condemnation for those in Christ. This was true for the Roman Christians, it's true for believers today, and it will always be true for God's kids. This isn't based on a person's actions, thoughts, or circumstances—it's based on the righteousness of Christ and faith in Him.

1. **Look up the word *condemnation* in a dictionary and summarize the definitions in your own words.**

Condemnation was the natural outcome of humanity's unrighteousness (Romans 3:1–20), but this fate no longer applied to those in Christ. And now, not only did Christ provide freedom from that punishment, but the Spirit also brought freedom from the mastery of sin and death, introducing believers to a new way of life.

★ 2. Look back at Day 5 of last week (Romans 7:21–25) and review the matching exercise with the different laws. Which three laws did Paul refer to in 8:2–4? In your own words, explain what they mean.

A.

B.

C.

Believers now live under a new law—the law of the Spirit of life. Jesus fulfilled the righteous requirement of the law *and* condemned sin, once for all. This opens up a new way of living, as believers are enabled to walk according to the Spirit.

**Review 8:5–8.**

Paul contrasted life according to the flesh with life according to the Spirit, and it all came down to what a person "set their mind on." In ancient Judaism, the mind didn't just refer to the intellect—it encapsulated the whole person: thoughts, desires, actions, and world view.

The goal wasn't for the Roman believers to spend all their time meditating on the Spirit. Instead, Paul was pointing them toward a lifestyle—one wholly anchored in and directed by God—which was a result of following the "law of the Spirit of life."

3. Fill in the table below with the implications of a mind set on the flesh and one set on the Spirit.

| Verse | Mind set on the flesh | Mind set on the Spirit |
| --- | --- | --- |
| 8:6 | | |
| 8:7 | | |
| 8:8 | | |

There's an important distinction between those who walk or live "according to the flesh" (8:4–5) and those who are "in the flesh" (8:8). It's possible for Christians to give in to their sinful desires—following the way of their flesh—and still be Christians. But those who are "in the flesh" are nonbelievers; they don't have the Holy Spirit dwelling in them.

**Review 8:9–11.**

4. **Take a look at 8:1–11 in the ESV.** How many times are *flesh* and *Spirit* mentioned?

Flesh:

Spirit:

5. According to 8:9, what is the proof of being "in the Spirit"? How many times does this phrase occur in 8:9–11?

Paul wasn't being redundant. He wanted his audience to understand the flesh was still a present reality in their lives. And so was the Spirit! Even though the flesh—the fallen human condition—continued to dwell with believers, the Spirit now also took up residence in them.

The body might be "dead because of sin" (8:10), but the closeness and intimacy of the Spirit provides the new life we all need—both in the present and in anticipation of the future. This is what gives believers hope, peace, and power as we seek to walk according to God's ways. We are not alone in this pursuit—the Spirit is with us!

In case Paul's audience needed a little more reassurance about the Spirit's capabilities in their lives, he provided them with an example.

6. What demonstrated the power of the Holy Spirit in 8:11?

That is good news! The Spirit dwelling in believers is proof of a new relationship with Christ. And if the Spirit could raise Jesus from the grave, He can powerfully work within us as we battle the flesh and await future resurrection life, like our Savior is already experiencing.

★ 7. In what ways do you struggle to walk according to the Spirit? How does the reminder of the Spirit's power and presence within you give you hope? Explain.

# Romans 8:12–17

 **READ ROMANS 8:12–17**

**Review 8:12–13.**

There are two main points in this section. First, Paul's audience was no longer under obligation to live according to fleshly desires. As he previously wrote, all thoughts, actions, and desires directed toward the flesh lead to death. Second, they should be active in the battle against the flesh—also referred to here as deeds of the body.

★ 1. What did Paul call the Roman Christians to do in 8:13? Who empowers this action?

Remember how many times the Spirit was referenced in 8:1–11? Well, He's nowhere near exiting the scene. Paul's understanding of the Christian life left no room for a "pull yourself up by your bootstraps" mentality. God did *all* the work to save us. He will continue to work in, alongside, and with us as we pursue life in the Spirit.

**Review 8:14–17.**

Believers are freed from the mastery of the flesh through the help of the Spirit—which is good news—but God doesn't stop there.

2. There are a number of familial words in this section. Write down as many as you can find in preparation for where Paul took his argument.

The Spirit not only leads us but also bestows a new identity on us through adoption: sons of God. Paul has taken his audience—and us—on quite a journey so far in the book of Romans. Even just to be free from the power and mastery of the flesh and sin might seem like enough, but God doesn't do the bare minimum. He does *so much more*.

3. Circle the descriptors Paul used for the Holy Spirit in 8:14–15.

Spirit of God

spirit of slavery

Spirit of adoption

Spirit of Jesus

Paul's audience, living in the Greco-Roman world, would've understood the privileges and rights associated with adoption. An adopted child received the same inheritance as a natural-born child. They experienced a new relationship as a son or daughter in a family. They were deliberately chosen. All debts incurred before their adoption were canceled. They received the same status as any natural-born children. And an adopted child was given a new name, which meant a new identity.

Paul used the Aramaic word for father (*abba*) alongside the Greek word for father (*patér*)—perhaps appealing to his Jewish and Gentile audience. This may remind you of Jesus's use of "Abba, Father" in His prayers. God's Son called Him Abba, and the Spirit of adoption helps us cry out to God in this same way.

★ 4. Which aspect(s) of Greco-Roman adoption (as described above) help you better understand your own reality as an adopted child of God?

If it's difficult to see yourself as God's beloved child, the Spirit actually serves as a witness to this truth. The Spirit reminds believers of their adoption, their truest and eternal identity, and all the blessings that come with it!

5. Match the statements from verses 16–17 to what you learned about adoption.

| | |
|---|---|
| Children of God | New relationship in a family |
| Heirs | All previous debts were canceled |
| Heirs of God | Same status as natural-born child |
| Fellow heirs with Christ | Inheritance |

Paul adds one caveat to adoption that wasn't associated with this ancient practice: suffering. It might've been nice if Paul ended this sentence with "fellow heirs with Christ." But suffering is a critical piece of the Christian life. Paul knew this, the Roman Christians knew this, and most likely, you know this too. Paul had more to say about suffering—which we'll look at tomorrow—but one thing is clear: We suffer with Jesus now and we'll be glorified with Him in the future.

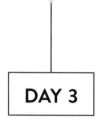

# Romans 8:18–25

 **READ ROMANS 8:18–25**

We ended yesterday's study with an introduction to a key theme Paul wove throughout the rest of this chapter: the reality of suffering.

**Review 8:18.**

1. Fill in the blanks in 8:18 below.

"For I _____ that the _____ of this _____ time are ____ _____

_____ with the _____ that is to be _____ to us."

Paul acknowledged the difficult but true reality of suffering in the present. He experienced great suffering and persecution—recorded in the book of Acts—and he knew that his friends in the Roman church suffered too. Like most believers in that day, they experienced persecution from Rome in addition to other difficult circumstances such as bad health, death, financial need, and relational strife. Paul and the Romans suffered in spite of, and sometimes because of, their new life in the Spirit.

We also know this to be true today—bad things happen to us, around us, sometimes through us as we battle sin, and even when we obey God. This reality didn't change Paul's conviction. None of the suffering, however bad, will even be comparable to the good that awaits us.

★ 2. As you consider your own situation or the suffering you see around you, what comes to mind when you read 8:18?

**Review 8:19–22.**

The truth is, all creation—not just humanity—longs, hopes, and looks forward to God making the world right again. No more sin, suffering, or death. Paul wrote as if creation were craning its neck to see just what God was going to do to bring about freedom and fix what had gone wrong.

He also used an interesting phrase—"groaning together in the pains of childbirth" (8:22)—which captured the anguish of the present situation alongside the hope and expectation for new life.

3. Circle the words Paul used to describe creation's anticipation in 8:19–22.

in hope     set free     obtain freedom
groaning     nonchalant     futility
apathetic

**Review 8:23.**

Paul repeated the word *groan* here, describing his response and the response of the Roman Christians. They too were waiting for God to bring the restoration and freedom He promised. He might've also had in mind the groaning of the Israelites while they were enslaved in Egypt (Exodus 2:23–25). According to Paul, a groan is the proper response to suffering, anticipation, and expectation.

4. What did 8:23 say they were waiting for?

You might be thinking, *Wait a second, Paul. I thought we'd covered this adoption thing? Weren't the Roman Christians already adopted into God's family? Isn't the same true for me?* The answer is yes and the full realization of this is still to come. Sometimes this tension is referred to as "the already and not yet." Paul addressed this concept previously in Romans 8. There are freedom from the mastery of sin and true life in the Spirit now (already). But sin is still present and active. Ultimate freedom from sin, death, and suffering comes through "the redemption of our bodies" (not yet).

★ 5. In your own words describe the theological concept of "the already and not yet." How have you experienced the challenge of living in this tension?

**Review 8:24–25.**

★ 6. **Look up the word *hope* (8:24) in a Greek lexicon.** Describe it in your own words.

Paul's hope was in the person of Jesus Christ because He proved to be the long-hoped-for Messiah of Israel. Paul was confident that salvation *had* come through Jesus. God's promises *had* been fulfilled in Him. Therefore the ultimate hope of Christ's return and glory was certain though still in the future. This was why Paul said it's not quite here yet. There would be no point in hoping if Paul and the Roman Christians were already experiencing this glorious new reality. But instead they were waiting, maybe suffering, and definitely groaning.

But Paul was confident. He knew the story and was certain of how it would end. God had already fulfilled promises, and because of this, Paul continued to hope—with patience.

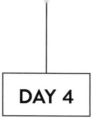

# Romans 8:26–30

 **READ ROMANS 8:26-30**

**Review 8:26–27.**

Paul connected the Spirit's intercession to yesterday's reading with a few key words: *likewise*, *weakness*, and *groanings*. The certainty that hope in Christ provided Paul and the Romans allowed them to wait with patience despite living in this "already and not yet." But as you know by this point in our study, God doesn't leave His children alone—the Spirit who dwells in believers is at work in all of us.

1. What were the two "problems" Paul and the Roman Christians dealt with in the waiting process? Do these feel true for you as well? Explain.

"Our weakness" could refer to the frailty of the human body—prone to sickness, death, and decay—or the difficulty of suffering. Paul likely had both in mind. Most importantly, he emphasized the role of the Spirit coming alongside "our weakness."

2. Write down the three actions of the Spirit in 8:26–27.

A.

B.

C.

No matter what is going on in your life right now, the Spirit is praying for you. The Spirit is in communication with God the Father (referred to here as "he who searches hearts"), groaning and interceding on behalf of God's people. He prayed for Paul when Paul was at a loss for words. He prayed for the believers in Rome. And He is praying for you. His prayers are not inconsequential, trivial, or flippant. They are personal, specific, and perfectly in line with the will of God.

**Review 8:28.**

Because the Spirit intercedes on behalf of believers (those who love God) according to the will of God, Paul can confidently say that all things work together for good. Remember, he had been writing about suffering, groaning, waiting, weakness, and difficulty in knowing how to pray.

But he also knew God called people according to His purpose: the ultimate redemption and restoration of all things. God's will and God's purpose will always be accomplished, both in our lives and in His larger salvation story.

★ 3. What "all things" are you currently hoping God works for good? How does the bigger context of this verse give you more confidence in the truth of this statement?

**Review 8:29–30.**

It's important to note the connecting word *for* in verse 29. Despite the truth of the previous statement, you might be wondering, *How exactly does God work all things for good according to His purpose—especially in the midst of suffering?* These verses answer this question.

★ 4. **Look up the following terms in a Bible dictionary or Greek lexicon.** Write the definition and then define the term using your own words.

| Terms | Bible dictionary definition | Definition in your own words |
|---|---|---|
| Foreknew (8:29) | | |
| Predestined (8:29) | | |
| Called (8:30) | | |
| Justified (8:30) | | |
| Glorified (8:30) | | |

Paul clarified that God had a specific purpose for those He predestined: "to be conformed to the image of his Son." God works through all our circumstances to make us like Jesus now so that we will also be like Jesus in the future.

The first four terms in the table refer to events that have already happened in the lives of believers. However, Paul also chose to write *glorified* in the past tense. Glorification has yet to take place, but according to God—who exists outside of time—it's as good as done. This brings assurance and comfort that God's previous work in saving you will mean ultimate redemption in glorification. It's already happened, and also, not yet.

# Romans 8:31–39

 READ ROMANS 8:31-39

In today's reading, Paul employs one of his favorite writing tools. Using the Greco-Roman rhetorical style, he asks seven questions.

**Review 8:31–35.**

The first question in this section demonstrated Paul's awe as he considered the grand scope of God's salvation—from the personal work in the lives of believers to the ultimate purposes of God. All God had done, all He is doing, and all He will certainly accomplish in the future led Paul to exclaim, "What then shall we say to these things?" The response is implied: *"Nothing! Nothing can be said to refute these truths."*

Reread 8:17–18 and 8:26. Suffering and the tension of "already and not yet" provided the context for this section of questions and answers. Believers live "in the Spirit" but also in bodies, which still experience the reality of sin and suffering. In the midst of this, the truth is "God is for us" and nothing can separate us from His love.

Unfortunately, these are the very things we can be inclined to doubt during difficult circumstances.

★ 1. Have there been times, past or present, when it's been difficult for you to believe these truths about God? Describe your experience.

Paul reminded the Roman Christians that in the midst of suffering, God was on their side. The implied answer to Paul's second question in 8:31 ("If God is for us, who can be against us?") was *"No one!"* God sent Jesus Christ to die on the cross to deal with sin, the very thing that separated humanity from God. This showed God's love. God's own Son provided salvation, fulfilling God's promises. We can be confident that in both the present and the future, God will provide everything believers need in order to one day be glorified with Him.

2. Based on what you've learned about justification, how would you explain Paul's answer in 8:33? **Look back to Romans 3 (Week 2, Day 3) for help.**

Romans 8 began with a powerful truth—no believer can be condemned—and Paul reminded the Romans of this here. There is no one who can condemn a follower of Christ, because Christ's death dealt with the guilt and punishment we all deserve.

As if this weren't enough, Jesus Christ is at the right hand of God praying for all of us! We've already learned the Holy Spirit intercedes for us, and here we see that Jesus also is praying for us. This led Paul to ask the next question: "Who shall separate us from the love of Christ?"

★ 3. List the things Paul mentioned in 8:35 that might be suggested as separating believers from the love of Christ. Write down any things you've experienced or are currently experiencing that could be added to this list.

**Review 8:36–37.**

The quote in 8:36 comes from Psalm 44. This psalm dealt with Israel's confusion and questions about God's love, deliverance, and faithfulness in the midst of their suffering. They were being obedient, yet they wondered if God had abandoned them.

You might also feel this way at times. Life is hard, things aren't as we think they should be, and some of the difficulties we experience can be due to our *obedience* to God. Paul and the Roman Christians certainly experienced this as well. The truth of God's love sometimes doesn't match the experience we have as Christians living in a fallen world.

Paul clarified this a bit in 8:37. When he referred to "all these things" he meant the list he wrote in 8:35 (including the personal things you added). Remember, our experience doesn't dictate God's love for us. Christ's death on the cross proved, once for all time, that God loves us!

4. Read through your list under today's third prompt. Now, go through it line by line and cross each item out as you remind yourself that *nothing* can separate you from God's love!

**Review 8:38–39.**

Just in case any doubt remained, Paul emphasized his point one more time, beginning with a declaration of his confidence: "I am sure."

5. What is the difference between the list in 8:35 and the list in 8:38?

God's love for believers—Paul, the Roman Christians, and us—has nothing to do with past circumstances, present trials, or powerful forces outside of our control. Our previous separation from God was dealt with on the cross by Christ Jesus our Lord. And nothing—*nothing*—can ever separate us from His love. He's where the joy is!

6. What stood out to you most in this week's study? Why?

7. What did you learn or relearn about God and His character this week?

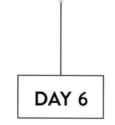

# Corresponding Psalm & Prayer

 **READ PSALM 44**

1. What correlation do you see between Psalm 44 and this week's study?

2. What portions of this psalm stand out to you most?

3. Close by praying this prayer aloud:

*Father,*
    *You've done great things for Your kids throughout history: loved us, created us, prayed for us, and saved us. In Your name, we've*

*boasted continually. Today I join in the song all Your kids—past, present, and future—are singing. I will give thanks to You forever.*

*As You know, God, I have suffered. Sometimes my suffering is tied into the consequences of my sin. Forgive me not only for my sin, but also for the suffering my sin has caused in my life and in the lives of others.*

*Other times, my suffering is a result of others' sins, or just the result of living in a fallen world. Sometimes it can be hard to tell what causes my suffering. So teach me when to repent and when to cry out for Your deliverance. Creation is groaning, Lord, and so am I. But because of Your unfailing and unending love, I can pray to You. And so I pray: Come quickly, Lord Jesus. And until the day when You do, fill me with hope.*

*While I wait on Your return, help me to set my mind—my thoughts, desires, actions, and world view—on You. May Your Spirit guide me in every minute of every day. I surrender my life to You, Lord—every moment of my day, each decision I make, I yield my will and way to Your perfect will and way.*

*I love You too. Amen.*

# Rest, Catch Up, or Dig Deeper

 **WEEKLY CHALLENGE**

Sin has marred and infiltrated every aspect of life. It can be difficult to imagine the future without it. But freedom from sin and all its effects is one of the many things we have to look forward to in our future. This is what gave Paul hope in Romans 8 (Days 3–5).

Try to picture a world free from sin—no angry outbursts, no need for medicine or police officers, no depression, no anxiety, no locks on doors, no one goes to bed hungry. Make two columns in your journal. In the left column, write the things you see in the world and in your own life that have been tainted by sin. In the right column, do your best to imagine the restoration and re-creation of a perfect world—either in words or with visual art. When the unknowns of the future feel frightening, let the right column give you hope.

**WEEK 6**

# Romans 9

┌─ Scripture to Memorize ─┐

For to set the mind on
the flesh is death, but
to set the mind on the
Spirit is life and peace.

Romans 8:6

## DAILY BIBLE READING

Day 1: Romans 9:1–5

Day 2: Romans 9:6–13

Day 3: Romans 9:14–18

Day 4: Romans 9:19–29

Day 5: Romans 9:30–33

Day 6: Psalm 75

Day 7: Catch-Up Day

**Corresponds to Day 343 of *The Bible Recap*.**

## WEEKLY CHALLENGE

See page 168 for more information.

# Romans 9:1–5

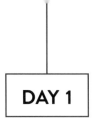 **READ ROMANS 9:1–5**

In 8:31–39, Paul taught that God's elect are inseparable from Him. Which leads to the question, Who are God's elect? Which leads to the question, Did they elect Him or did He elect them? And so we begin our study of Romans 9, one of the most highly contested chapters in the Bible.

With any complex issue concerning who God is, it's good to dig and to wrestle. But in doing so, if you come to a different conclusion from that of fellow believers, look for the things that unify, not divide. We can disagree, in humility and love, with our brothers and sisters and still be brothers and sisters.

Before we study this difficult and important chapter together, let's pray.

*Father, You are sovereign and You are good. Your ways are unsearchable, but You come near to us. Your thoughts are a mystery, but You make Yourself known to us. You created us in Your image; stop us from attempting to create You in ours. Guide us as we dig into and wrestle with Your Word. Give us a spirit of humility and unity. Amen.*

**Review 9:1–3.**

1. Why is Paul heartbroken?

Paul's love for his fellow ethnic Jews was undeniable here. Like Moses when he pled to the Lord on behalf of the golden-calf-worshiping Israelites (Exodus 32:32), Paul wished he could take their place if doing so meant they would come to know Christ.

★ 2. Does your heart break for those who don't know Christ? Think of someone whom you love and who is an unbeliever and write their initials below. If you aren't already doing so regularly, commit to pray for their salvation every day this week.

**Review 9:4–5.**

Paul reminded the Roman Christians of the special relationship God had with Israel throughout history, full of privileges and promises.

★ 3. Match the event and reference on the left with the corresponding summary on the right.

| Event and Reference | Summary |
|---|---|
| The Adoption (Exodus 4:22) | God fulfilled His promises to the Israelites through generations, showing His consistent character. |
| The Glory (2 Chronicles 7:1–3) | God established a covenant with David that from his lineage would come the eternal King. |
| The Covenant (2 Samuel 7:12–13) | The glory of the LORD filled the temple. |
| The Giving of the Law (Leviticus 20:7–8; Exodus 19:5) | By giving Israel the gift of and instructions for worship, God reminded them of His special relationship with them. |
| The Worship (Psalm 135:3–4) | God gave Israel the law to reveal Himself and set them apart. |
| The Promises (Joshua 23:14) | From their lineage came Jesus, the Promised Messiah. |
| The Patriarchs (Exodus 3:15) | God called Israel His son. |
| The First Coming of Christ (Matthew 1:1) | None of God's promises to Israel ever failed. |

Throughout history God's people had front-row seats to what He was doing. Every event you just read about, every Scripture you just looked up—and so many more events and Scriptures—pointed to Jesus. Before God opened his eyes to this truth, Paul was blind to it (Acts 26:9–23). But after his conversion, the truth about Jesus became the corrective lens through which he understood the entire world. *It all made sense because of Jesus.* And he was heartbroken that his Jewish brothers didn't see it too. But even in his anguish, he ended with a reminder about God's character.

4. How did Paul describe Christ in 9:5? Fill in the blanks below.

"…from their race, according to the flesh, is the Christ, who is _____ _____

_____, blessed forever. Amen."

God is sovereign over everything and everyone. As Christ-followers with a right view of God and of ourselves, His sovereignty shouldn't make us scared or angry. It should make us bless His name in worship and praise forever. Amen!

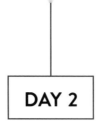

# Romans 9:6–13

✝ **READ ROMANS 9:6-13**

Paul knew his Jewish audience would be wondering, *God made these promises to us. If they don't include us, then haven't His promises failed?* To prove his unequivocal *"No,"* Paul reminded them of two familiar stories from two of their ancestors, Isaac and Jacob. If you aren't familiar with these stories or want a refresher, Isaac's is found in Genesis 16–18 and 21. Jacob's is in Genesis 25–27.

**Review 9:6–7.**

As we studied in Romans 2 and 4, unbelieving Jews thought that simply being Abraham's descendants made them God's people. Again, Paul corrected their thinking, and here, he used their own patriarchs to do so.

1. **Read Genesis 21:12.** What did God tell Abraham about Isaac? What did God tell Abraham about Ishmael, "the slave woman's" (Hagar's) son?

**Review 9:8–9.**

Both Ishmael and Isaac were sons of Abraham, but both were not "children of Abraham" (9:7). God's promise to Abraham to bless all families of the earth through him (Genesis 12:1–3) required the inclusion of his wife, Sarah (Genesis 17:15–21). So Ishmael, the son Abraham had with Hagar, wasn't a part of that promise. In a broader sense, Paul was basically saying, *"Look, if Abraham's own child wasn't even a child of the promise, what makes you think that because Abraham is your great-great-great-great-grandfather, you're automatically a child of the promise?"*

And in case one patriarchal example wasn't enough, Paul reminded them of Jacob.

2. **Read Genesis 25:19–24.** What did God tell Rebekah about the twins in her womb?

**Review 9:10–12.**

Jacob was younger than his twin brother, Esau, but before they were even born, God chose Jacob to be called Israel (Genesis 32:28). Jacob struggled with God, then came to be governed by Him, and the promise God gave to Abraham was extended through Jacob/Israel (Genesis 35:9–12).

Some theologians say that Paul referred here to the nations of Israel (from Jacob) and Edom (from Esau). That's possible. Through that lens, Esau/Edom was blessed in many ways (Genesis 33:9 and 36). And Jacob/Israel was blessed in more: with the adoption, the glory, the covenants, the law, the worship, the promises, and the Messiah (Romans 9:4–5).

But other theologians point out that Paul was also referring to people here, and therefore, he wasn't just talking about God's election of nations, but of *individuals*. This was hard for Paul's fellow Jews to hear, and it's hard for many of us to hear today too. So let's look at a few other places in both the Old and New Testaments that address it.

★ 3. **Look up the verses below.** Write what they say about God's election.

| Reference | Teaching about election |
|---|---|
| Exodus 33:19 NIV | |
| Deuteronomy 7:6 | |
| Isaiah 46:10 | |
| John 15:16 | |
| Ephesians 1:3–6 | |

★ 4. What do all these verses teach?

**Review 9:13.**

To wrap up his examples, Paul quoted God's words from the prophet Malachi: "Yet I have loved Jacob but Esau I have hated" (Malachi 1:2–3). In the Old Testament, the Hebrew word *hated—śānē'*—meant "to detest something or someone." But when Paul wrote his letter to the Romans in Greek, he used the word *miseō*. Its meaning is a little less clear. In some places, it means "to detest" (Luke 21:17), while in others it means "to prefer less" (Luke 14:26). Whichever meaning is closer to Paul's intent here, this truth does not change: God is righteous and He is holy. We all deserve to be detested; we all deserve His wrath. Sparing any of us is His mercy. Loving any of us is His grace.

In the examples Paul gave today, there are two important things to notice. First, in both examples, there were elements of human responsibility: Abraham took a woman who wasn't his wife. Esau sold his birthright. The Bible doesn't pit God's sovereignty against human responsibility; if anything does that, it's our misguided theology.

And second, in both examples, the natural order of things was turned upside down: The second-born was treated like the first. Through these examples—and many more—God's been pointing to this all along: The last will be first.

So why was this hard for some Jews to understand or accept? And why is it hard for some people to understand or accept now? Human nature is such that we love an underdog—unless we're the presumptive winner. We must have a right view of God and of ourselves. We aren't elected because of our heritage. We aren't elected because of our own good works. We are elected "because of Him who calls" us (9:11). Praise God!

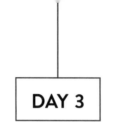

DAY 3

# Romans 9:14–18

### ✠ READ ROMANS 9:14-18

Some believers struggle with teachings about God's election because it feels unjust—maybe not for themselves, but for someone they love who isn't yet a believer. Perhaps you've shared the gospel with a family member who has rejected it or even grown angry toward you; you've prayed for them fervently. You've done all you can do, yet their heart has not changed. Paul understood your ache. Remember his heartbreak for his fellow Jews as he began this chapter? So Paul, as he has done many times before, anticipated this struggle and asked the question for his audience: "Is there injustice on God's part?" (9:14).

**Review 9:14.**

1. Complete the table below with Paul's emphatic answer from the listed English translations.

| Greek | ESV | NIV | NLT | NKJV | KJV |
|---|---|---|---|---|---|
| *me ginomai* | By no means! | | | | |

Paul proved his answer by focusing not on justice, but on mercy. Absolutely no one has or ever will deserve to be saved by God. If we insist on what we deserve, we insist on sending ourselves to hell. Salvation is unfair. And it's unfair on the side of mercy, because God is merciful.

**Review 9:15–16.**

While God met with Moses on Mount Sinai and gave him the tablets of the law, the Israelites were busy making a golden calf and worshiping it. Upon seeing their sin against the God who'd just brought them out of slavery, Moses threw the tablets, breaking them into pieces (Exodus 32:1–20).

God's law was a gift to His people that revealed Himself and showed them the right way to live. When they decided to go their own way and worship an object they created, God could have left them to their own devices. But He didn't.

★ 2. **Read Exodus 34:1–7.** What did God do? What did God say about Himself?

God chose to have mercy on Israel. They deserved death, but He spared them. His mercy was His to give freely; and when given after such a betrayal from Israel, the beauty of His mercy shone all the brighter. Not only did God not give Israel what they did deserve, but He gave them grace, which is what they *didn't* deserve. He gave them new tablets of the law, a renewed covenant, and a reassurance of the special relationship they had with Him.

We often think of mercy and grace as synonyms, but they're closer to opposites that work together. Today, God's mercy and grace are still His to give freely. He's given you, as a believer, His mercy—sparing you from what you deserve. And He's also given you His grace—blessing you with what you don't deserve.

And just as He has done it for you, and just as He did it for Paul when Paul was on a mission to persecute and murder Christians, He can do it for your loved ones who don't know Him—even those who are sprinting away from Him like Paul was. Paul wasn't seeking God, but God was seeking Paul. Paul deserved death, but God had (and has) mercy. When all hope seems lost, His loving mercy remains our greatest hope!

3. Match the passages below with some of the gifts of grace that God has given believers.

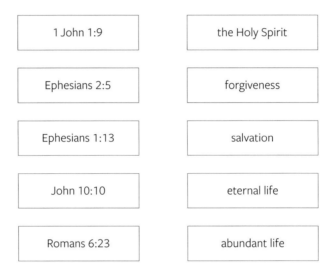

| | |
|---|---|
| 1 John 1:9 | the Holy Spirit |
| Ephesians 2:5 | forgiveness |
| Ephesians 1:13 | salvation |
| John 10:10 | eternal life |
| Romans 6:23 | abundant life |

★ 4. What other gifts of grace has God given you?

**Review 9:17–18.**

Using another Exodus example, Paul reminded his audience that God even used Pharaoh to display His mercy and grace through the Israelites. God put Pharaoh on the Egyptian throne and God hardened Pharaoh's heart. Why?

5. **Read Exodus 7:1–5 in the NLT.** Complete the end of each sentence below.

I will make Pharaoh's heart stubborn so →

I raise my powerful hand and bring out the Israelites →

When God hardened Pharaoh's heart, it led to a chain of events that showed God's power—not just to the ancient Israelites and not just to the ancient Egyptians, but to nations around the world, throughout generations. In Sunday school classrooms this week, children will learn about how God split wide the sea, poured water from a rock, and rained manna from the sky. Pharaoh's hardness served to proclaim God's power, mercy, and grace.

These are hard things to grasp sometimes, and it's an act of faith to praise God even for the things we don't yet fully understand. These stories show us aspects of His character, revealing His heart and His ways to humankind. His ways are not like ours, and sometimes they're beyond our complete understanding—but it's worthwhile to seek to know and understand Him more than we currently do. As we seek to know Him more, we can love and trust Him more. Like Asaph wrote, even "the wrath of man shall praise" Him (Psalm 76:10)!

# Romans 9:19–29

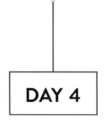 **READ ROMANS 9:19-29**

The next question Paul anticipated was essentially *"Then why does God blame people?"* Or *"If God gives mercy, and He wills who He gives it to, and people can't resist His will, then why would He fault anyone for not being recipients of His mercy?"*

**Review 9:19–20.**

1. **Read Job 38:1–5.** What similarities do you notice between God's answer to Job and Paul's answer to his audience?

Paul's tone in answering this question was a bit different from what we've seen so far. As a teacher, Paul welcomed genuine questions. And as an apostle, Paul reminded us all of our place. We are the limited, weak, sinful creation. God is the infinite, almighty, perfect Creator. With our questions about Him, we must remember who He is and who we are.

**Review 9:21.**

If you've ever seen a potter shape vessels, you know that what starts out as a wet pile of mud can—with skill, care, and time—be turned into a work of art. As the potter, God picks up some of the mud and turns it into something beautiful, shaping it to be more like Himself and setting it apart to be with Him forever. And isn't that the potter's right?

Paul might've been scolding his audience a bit in this section, but he was never flippant or unkind. He used a style of teaching here that reminds us of Jesus.

2. Read the passages below and take notes about them. What do they all have in common?

| Matthew 6:25–27 | Luke 6:32–36 | Romans 9:20–21 |
|---|---|---|
|  |  |  |
| **What do they all have in common?** | | |
|  | | |

**Review 9:22–24.**

In these verses, your Bible translation might have another question that begins with "What if," but the Greek statement uses *de*, which is closer to "but," or "moreover." Paul answered the question in 9:19 with something like this: *"God is longsuffering with the vessels of destruction. In doing so, the glory of His mercy shines all the brighter."*

A vase on its own can be beautiful. But a vase compared to the pile of mud it came from is breathtaking. God endures with the mud, giving it a place to exist. But it is still mud.

God endures with sinners. He gives them a place to exist and gives them common grace such as air, rain, health, and even success. But the sin continues, and sometimes it's almost too depraved to bear. Against that backdrop, God elected some of the sinners to become saints, paying for their redemption with His Son. Make no mistake, vessels prepared for destruction are prepared by man's sin. But vessels prepared for glory are prepared by God's mercy and grace.

This is an important note: These teachings are not a call for self-loathing, shame, or despair. They're an opportunity to relish in God's great love for you! The apostle Peter explained God's merciful patience with humanity this way: "The Lord is not slow to fulfill his promise as some count slowness, but is patient toward you, not wishing that any should perish, but that all should reach repentance" (2 Peter 3:9). And in the Old Testament, King David explained God's beautiful grace this way: "The LORD is merciful and gracious, slow to anger and abounding in steadfast love. . . . As far as the east is from the west, so far does he remove our transgressions from us" (Psalm 103:8, 12).

**Review 9:25–29.**

Paul closed this section with two additional examples of God's mercy and grace.

★ 3. Read Isaiah 1:9 (NLT) below. How is this an example of God's mercy?

> "If the LORD of Heaven's Armies had not spared a few of us,
> we would have been wiped out like Sodom, destroyed like Gomorrah."

★ 4. Read God's words from Hosea 2:23 (NLT) below. How is this an example of His grace?

> "I will show love to those I called 'Not loved.'
> And to those I called 'Not my people,' I will say, 'Now you are my people.'
> And they will reply, 'You are our God!'"

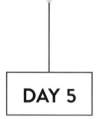

# Romans 9:30–33

 **READ ROMANS 9:30–33**

Sometimes, when we study difficult passages of Scripture, we're so focused on the details that we miss the big picture. And sometimes, we're looking so hard for the big picture that we misunderstand the details. So before we wrap up this week's study, let's pause to review both.

1. Which of the following details has Paul taught so far in Romans 9? Put a check mark by all that are true.

- ☐ Don't bother sharing the gospel because God only elects a few people.
- ☐ God elected Jacob before he was born in order that God's purpose of election might continue.
- ☐ God elects the people who work the hardest.
- ☐ God has mercy on whomever He wills and hardens whomever He wills.
- ☐ There is no such thing as human accountability.

★ 2. In your own words, what is the big picture of what Paul has been teaching in Romans 9?

Paul anticipated the final question of this chapter, one most of us would probably ask if given the chance: *"What does this mean?"*

**Review 9:30–33.**

In a summary statement that reemphasized his earlier teaching, Paul reminded the Romans that many in Israel were so focused on pursuing every detail of the law to prove their own righteousness that they missed the big picture: *Christ Himself is their righteousness.*

3. Read Isaiah 8:14. Draw a picture of the stone from this example.

We stumble over things we don't clearly see or comprehend, like the futility of our own self-righteousness. For many of Paul's fellow Jews, the fact that their righteousness was based in Christ and not in their own works was too much. Jesus became to them a stone they stumbled over.

But that's not the only image the Bible gives us of Christ as a stone.

4. Read Isaiah 28:16. Draw a picture of the stone from this example.

For some, Christ is the stone over which they stumble. For others, He's the rock upon which everything stands.

This is a bit of a spoiler, but after a week of study as intense and difficult as this one, a breath of fresh air is warranted. A *doxology* is a short outburst of praise, and in Romans 11:33, Paul wrote, "Oh, the depth of the riches and wisdom and knowledge of God! How unsearchable are his judgments and how inscrutable his ways!"

Faithful, thoughtful, prayerful theologians disagree about the implications of Romans 9 and how it works out today in individuals' salvation. We can study and search and pray—and we should!—but God's wisdom and knowledge are deeper and richer than we can fully understand. On Day 1 of this week, you prayed, *Your ways are unsearchable, but You come near to us. Your thoughts are a mystery, but You make Yourself known to us.*

He's sovereign. He's merciful. He's gracious. He's good. And He's where the joy is!

5. What stood out to you most in this week's study? Why?

6. What did you learn or relearn about God and His character this week?

# Corresponding Psalm & Prayer

✝ **READ PSALM 75**

1. What correlation do you see between Psalm 75 and this week's study?

2. What portions of this psalm stand out to you most?

3. Close by praying this prayer aloud:

*Father,*
*You are merciful and gracious, slow to anger, abounding in stead-*
*fast love and faithfulness. You are righteous, perfect, and holy. I'm*

*in awe of the wonderful things You've done. I will declare it forever: The God of Jacob/Israel cuts off the wicked but lifts up the righteous.*

*Without You, I was also wicked. You alone make me righteous, but I still struggle with understanding who You are. Instead of relishing in the depth of the riches and wisdom and knowledge of You, I've scoffed at things I don't fully understand. I've been angry or frustrated when Your ways seem harsh. At times, I've insisted that You fit into the box I've created for You, and I've dismissed any theology that tears the box apart. Or I've twisted the good, true, and beautiful aspects of Your character and I've used them as excuses for my sin. Forgive me, Lord.*

*Remind me always that You've chosen to show me compassion. You've chosen to have mercy on me. You've chosen to give me grace. Because You have called me, I am saved.*

*I surrender my life to You, Lord—every moment of my day, each decision I make, I yield my will and way to Your perfect will and way.*

*I love You too. Amen.*

**DAY 7**

# Rest, Catch Up, or Dig Deeper

On Day 5, we learned that a doxology is a short outburst of praise. It comes from the Greek words *doxa* (which means "glory") and *logos* (which means "word"). Write your own doxology praising God for both what you understand about Him and what you don't.

# Romans 10–11

┌─ **Scripture to Memorize** ─┐

For the mind that is set on the flesh is hostile to God, for it does not submit to God's law; indeed, it cannot. Those who are in the flesh cannot please God.

Romans 8:7–8

## DAILY BIBLE READING

Day 1: Romans 10:1–4

Day 2: Romans 10:5–21

Day 3: Romans 11:1–10

Day 4: Romans 11:11–24

Day 5: Romans 11:25–36

Day 6: Psalm 30

Day 7: Catch-Up Day

Corresponds to Days 343 and 344 of *The Bible Recap.*

## WEEKLY CHALLENGE

See page 197 for more information.

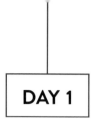

# DAY 1

# Romans 10:1–4

 **READ ROMANS 10:1–4**

**Review 10:1.**

1. How did Paul address his audience?

2. What plural pronoun did he use to refer to the unbelieving Jews?

While this may have felt like exclusive language—an "us versus them" mentality—notice Paul's heart about the situation. Right away, his audience understood the magnitude of this separation. He wasn't arrogant about being in the family of God, and there were no boasts about who's in and who's out—there was only a deep brokenness over the lostness of Israel.

★ 3. **Look back at 9:3.** What would Paul do if he could? What does this say about his heart for the lost?

This young church had experienced its fair share of division. The Roman church and pockets of believers all over the world were meshing together, sorting out their differences in order to be drawn together in unity. This was not an easy task—and it's one the global church is still working out today. So rather than speaking of the unbelieving Jews as outsiders, Paul spoke of them with a deep longing in his heart, pouring himself out in prayer for their salvation.

4. Can you sense the longing Paul felt? Do you experience the same depth of grief over the lost? In the space below, write a prayer asking God to broaden your circle to reach the lost. And most importantly, ask Him to create a desire in your heart for their salvation.

Israel's salvation wasn't up to Paul, but that didn't stop him from praying, and it didn't stop him from sharing the gospel. In fact, sharing the gospel was his life focus. Saving the lost isn't in our power, but praying for them and reaching out to them *is* our responsibility.

Paul's fervent prayer for his countrymen showed that there was still hope for Israel. They had not fallen beyond repair. Paul himself was a perfect example of a changed heart. As we'll see in Romans 11, God does have a plan for Israel. He will provide the ultimate proof of His faithfulness when He fulfills His promise to this nation.

**Review 10:2.**

5. As Paul could attest to, what did Israel have going for them?

Without a doubt, the Jews were passionate about the ordinances of God. Few could hold a candle to their knowledge of the Scriptures, their memorization of the Mosaic law, or their adherence to its practices. But none of that matters when your heart is darkened to the love, compassion, and grace of God. They had knowledge—but their knowledge lacked true understanding.

In John 5, when Jesus spoke to the Pharisees (the religious leaders of the day), He explained that the Scriptures they zealously pored over pointed to Him as their long-awaited Messiah. He even went so far as to question whether they believed the writings of Moses.

6. **Read John 5:46 and fill in the blanks.**

"For if you believed Moses, you would believe ____; for ____ wrote of ____."

In essence, they missed the entire point.

**Review 10:3.**

7. What word did Paul use to describe the Jews' state of mind toward the righteousness of God?

Paul was not being offensive. He simply meant that they hadn't recognized and received the righteousness of God through the finished work of Jesus. Instead, they'd tried to compensate by creating their own. They were so steeped in their own self-righteousness that they were unwilling to submit to the very belief that would have saved them. "Professing to be wise, they became fools" (Romans 1:22 NKJV).

★ 8. Have you been there? Are you in that place now? Are you still "seeking to establish" your own righteousness despite belonging to Christ? Why do you think Christians still struggle with believing they have approval from God?

**Review 10:4.**

Paul made an important distinction here regarding the function of the law.

**9. Fill in the blanks from 10:4.**

"For Christ is the end of the law for _____ to everyone who believes."

The law is still very real. It's an important guide, but it is not—and never has been—the means for righteousness. Old Testament saints weren't saved by adhering to the law; they were saved by faith too (see Hebrews 11 for plenty of examples). And as we've seen from Abraham's example in Romans 4, Christ's sacrifice allows us to rest in grace. If you struggle with trying to attain your own righteousness to please God or obtain His favor, consider this an invitation to silence your inner Pharisee, believe God, and rest in His promises!

# Romans 10:5–21

### ✝ READ ROMANS 10:5–21

Yesterday's study ended with an often-misunderstood concept about the Old Testament and the rituals and laws God called the Israelites to follow. Here, Paul provided some clarity. And to help his first-century audience understand the cohesive story of the Bible, he almost exclusively used the Old Testament to make his points.

**Review 10:5–8.**

In 10:5, Paul referenced Leviticus 18:5, "You shall therefore keep my statutes and my rules; if a person does them, he shall live by them: I am the LORD." The clarification comes when paired with Deuteronomy 9:6, "Know, therefore, that the LORD your God is not giving you this good land to possess because of *your righteousness*, for you are a stubborn people" (emphasis added).

When God said they "shall live by" these statutes, He did not mean it would grant them salvation. He simply meant this was to be their guide for following Him. As Moses said in Deuteronomy, their deliverance wasn't because of their righteousness. It was the Lord's work—not their works—that brought them into the land.

1. Recall what we've learned so far about Abraham and where our righteousness comes from (4:3). Summarize in your own words below.

2. In 10:6–8, Paul interprets a portion of the Old Testament, but his wording gets a bit confusing, so use the table below to sort things out.

| Old Testament Passage | New Testament Passage | Paul's Parenthetical Statement |
|---|---|---|
| Deuteronomy 30:12 | Romans 10:6 | That is to bring Christ down |
| Deuteronomy 30:13 | Romans 10:7 | |
| Deuteronomy 30:14 | Romans 10:8 | |

To summarize, Paul's point was that eternal life has always been about a heart belief in Jesus. It's not about your achievements (the primary misconception of the law-abiding Jews) or being good enough (the primary misconception of nearly everyone else).

Whether you feel morally exceptional or like a dismal failure before God, that is not where your righteousness is lost or found. Even at your worst, you are no less loved and redeemed. We walk closely to God's moral law because it is the overflow of true faith in our hearts. To desire a righteous life is good and right, but its shadow side is a drift toward self-condemnation when we sin.

★ 3. To which end of that spectrum do you gravitate? Do you tend toward striving to prove something to God? Or toward thoughts of self-defeat and questioning your status with Him?

**Review 10:9–13.**

4. Write 10:9 below. Underline the two actions for the believer, then circle the two parts of the body.

5. According to 10:10, what is the outcome of these actions?

What we say out loud is an overflow of what we believe in our hearts. These are not magic words or an incantation for salvation. We speak it, or outwardly express it, because we believe it. "For out of the abundance of the heart his mouth speaks" (Luke 6:45).

Notice how many times Paul uses inclusive language in these verses. "Everyone who believes" (10:11), "the same Lord is Lord of all" (10:12), "all who call on him" (10:12), "everyone who calls on the name of the Lord will be saved" (10:13). These truths are from the prophets Isaiah and Joel; once again, Paul intentionally used Old Testament language to pull the cohesive story into the frame and remind his audience that salvation is available to everyone.

**Review 10:14–21.**

★ 6. Based on 10:14–17, what might be a second reason it's important that we "confess with our mouth"?

Romans 9 might've left you with questions about who will be saved and how or why God elects those He elects. But Romans 10 unquestioningly puts the responsibility on believers to go and tell. Paul quotes Isaiah 53:1, "Lord, who has believed what he has heard from us?" Like Isaiah, we don't know the answer to that question. Only God does. Therefore, we *must* share the word of Christ.

In fact, for some deeper study, take a look at Acts 9 to see why Romans 10:20 (quoting Isaiah 65:1) especially resonated with the author of our letter.

To close, 10:18–20 touched on a concept we will cover more in Romans 11. There is a circular plan at hand between Jews and Gentiles. We know that God commanded the gospel first be taken to the Jews and then to the Gentiles (1:16), but the book of Acts is a case study of how the disobedience of Israel opened the door for salvation to the Gentiles. Here, we see that the Gentiles' salvation created a soul-saving jealousy in the hearts of the Jews.

7. According to 10:21, what was God's action toward this disobedient and contrary people?

Whether people accept Him or reject Him, our job remains the same: Never tire of reaching the lost. Paul modeled this for us as well, being one of the chief missionaries of the first-century church. And his tireless efforts to share the gospel with the lost spread across the millennia, throughout the nations, and to us today!

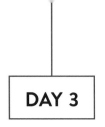

# Romans 11:1–10

## ⊕ READ ROMANS 11:1–10

Disobedient and contrary to the righteousness of God—that was the image we had of Israel as we closed Romans 10. However, lest we think that was reason enough for God to give up on His people—as though God were scrambling to come up with plan B because of their disobedience—Paul used Romans 11 to assure us there has always been a glorious future for Israel and that God will be faithful to see it through.

**Review 11:1–3.**

1. What was Paul's response to his own question in 11:1? Do you remember the Greek phrase? (Hint: Go back to our study on 3:4 or 9:14.)

Paul used himself as an example that God had not rejected Israel as a people. He knew the power of God unto salvation for all who believe (1:16)—even for a hardened heart like his.

2. Why was Paul such a good example of God's faithfulness to the Jews?

His testimony was a great example for the people of that time and place, but he also knew it was important for his audience to see God's consistency in the Old Testament. This was part of their heritage—even at their worst, God never let go of Israel.

The prophet Elijah was God's messenger to Israel during the time of King Ahab, a despicable, wicked leader in Israel's dark history. Elijah, despite having just won a fiery showdown with Ahab's pagan prophets (1 Kings 18–19), was depressed, desperate, and running for his life.

3. What reasons did Elijah give the Lord for feeling so hopeless (11:3)?

4. Who is the "they" in Elijah's story?

As we were reminded in Romans 9, God is sovereign. He certainly knew how bad things had gotten, and His heart was grieved over unrepentant Israel, much more than Elijah's. However, God knew something Elijah didn't know.

**Review 11:4–6.**

5. Pop quiz #1: Without looking at your Bible, how many men did God say He had kept for Himself?

    A. 17,000

    B. 7,000

    C. 700

    D. None of the above

6. Using context clues, how would you define the term *remnant*?

7. Pop quiz #2: What did God say about the men He had preserved?

    A. They perfectly kept the Levitical law.

    B. They had never bowed to the pagan god Baal.

    C. Some of them honored Him but others didn't.

God never said these men were perfect. It wasn't their squeaky-clean record that qualified them to be part of His redemptive plan for Israel. The one thing they had going for them was that they had never bowed to Baal. God's plan was unmoved because it was—and always will be—based on His character, not ours. God said *He* is the one who kept them for Himself.

8. In 11:5–6, Paul drove home a point that was applicable then and is applicable now. Write these verses below and circle the word *grace* every time it appears.

As the Holy Spirit prompted Paul to write this section, He gave us an opportunity to learn more about His character. He is a God of grace. He exists outside of time and space, and He knows every person who would hear or read this passage. He knew some of these doctrines would be difficult to understand and even harder to swallow. But what this passage makes abundantly clear is that He is the picture of grace toward humanity.

In Romans 9, the Holy Spirit had Paul use another word on this topic of redemption: *mercy*. As we've discussed, grace and mercy are not interchangeable, but they work together to give us a truer picture of God's kindness toward us.

In His *mercy*, God spares us from what we deserve: His wrath. In His *grace*, He not only spares us from His wrath but gives us what we do not deserve: eternal life with Him.

★ 9. Pop quiz #3: Without looking back, write definitions for *grace* and *mercy* below.

Grace:

Mercy:

★ 10. How are they similar? How are they different?

★ 11. Considering your own not-so-squeaky-clean record, how does this truth about God's character bring you comfort?

**Review 11:7–10.**

Paul urged his audience to heed the same word of warning that his Old Testament predecessors gave: Beware a hardened heart. God's hardening of Israel's heart was adjacent to their disobedience. They sought their own path of righteousness instead of God's way; only the elect (those whom God, in His mercy, chose to spare) were able to receive His righteousness.

These quotes Paul borrowed from Moses and David are just the tip of the Old Testament iceberg on warnings to Israel—but Israel was deaf to God's instruction. Thankfully, their deaf ears and hardened hearts did not have the final say in God's plan.

You are in this study because you desire to have ears to hear what the gracious and merciful Holy Spirit has to say to your heart. But you are also here, being sanctified by the Word, because God chose to preserve a faithful remnant.

12. Close today by giving glory to God. Thank Him for His grace and mercy in bringing you into His redemptive plan.

# Romans 11:11–24

## ✝ READ ROMANS 11:11–24

If you're a Gentile (a non-Jew), you may not think much about Israel's past, present, or future or how it applies to you. But we'll see today how God's plan for Israel intersects with the Gentiles and how His faithfulness to all believers is revealed.

**Review 11:11–12.**

1. How would you describe the difference between stumbling and falling?

When the Old Testament prophets foretold this stumbling that would happen in Israel, they didn't mean the nation had been permanently cut off from God. Despite being unwilling to confess Jesus as the Messiah, Israel wouldn't be cut off from God forever—their rejection was not total, nor was it final. However, Israel's stumbling—their trespass—would be used by God to expand His kingdom to include "all nations" (see Genesis 18:18 and Isaiah 49:6).

2. How will the Gentiles' faith be used to attract the Jewish people to Jesus?

While Israel was called to be a light to the Gentiles (Isaiah 49), Gentiles would function as a light for Israel—for now.

Israel's rejection of the Messiah opened wide the doors for the gospel to other nations. While their failure lit a candle for the Gentiles' darkness, their repentance and restoration will turn on the floodlights, illuminating the whole world with the gospel!

★ 3. How does this affect the way you pray for the Jewish people? How does it create anticipation and excitement for the salvation of any Jewish people who haven't put their faith in Jesus?

**Review 11:13–16.**

Here, Paul turned his attention to the Gentiles in the audience. Every time you see the word *you* in the remainder of today's study, remember that Paul is referring to all non-Jews.

4. What emotion did Paul long to stir in his kinsmen (fellow ethnic Jews)?

Usually, when we're trying to make someone jealous, we have a malicious intent for selfish gain. But Paul's desire was different; he hoped their jealousy would be a catalyst for their salvation, leading to the full restoration of God's kingdom.

With his "lump of dough" metaphor, Paul referenced a command given to the Israelites in Numbers 15 when they entered the promised land. The first of their dough was to be presented to the Lord, thus consecrating the whole loaf. The application here is that Israel's faithful remnant is simply the firstfruits of Israel's salvation.

**Review 11:17–20.**

Paul used a beautiful illustration for the merging of these two worlds—Jews and Gentiles.

5. Using 11:17–18, label the parts of the olive tree and the wild olive shoot below with its corresponding people. (Remember who "you" is in this passage.)

**Olive Tree**

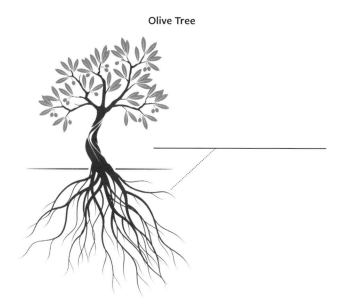

**Wild Olive Shoot**

Grafting is a process in which an olive farmer can graft a shoot from one tree into the branch of another tree—it can even be a different variety of olive tree. But first, a branch from the host tree must be cut off. Then the new shoot can be attached to the broken branch and begin absorbing its nutrients. The new branch doesn't replace the existing tree, it simply becomes a part of it. Interestingly, through grafting, two different types of olives can grow from one root.

★ 6. In your own words, what did Paul explain through this illustration?

In 11:19–20, Paul addressed any notion of superiority that the Gentiles might think they have over the Jews. Yes, God, in His grace, made a way for the Gentiles, but it wasn't because they had done anything to deserve it. And God's promise to ethnic Israel was still fully intact.

**Review 11:21–24.**

Some struggle with the meaning of 11:21–22, taking it to mean that you can lose your salvation. But look back at 11:20.

7. Why was Israel broken off? And how can the Gentiles stand fast?

8. Write 1 John 2:19 below. Combining this truth with Romans 11:21–22, why would anyone be "broken off" or "go out from us"?

This is not a passage about losing your salvation. It's a passage about exposing a phony faith.

9. According to 11:23, who has the power to restore?

The enemy of your soul may try to convince you that the road to Christ is too far—that you, or someone you love, is too far gone. But that is false. God is able to restore and redeem. No one is too far from God for Him to rescue them. And who better to testify to this than Paul himself?

And as for Israel, this root will one day thrive again.

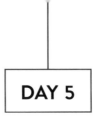

# Romans 11:25–36

 **READ ROMANS 11:25-36**

**Review 11:25–27.**

Continuing his idea that the Gentiles should not think themselves superior to the Jews, Paul reminded his audience that this hardness of Jewish hearts is simply the holding pattern until Israel is restored.

1. What did Paul say must happen before Israel will be saved?

Some of the smartest minds in religion and theology disagree on what "the fullness of the Gentiles" means. And in fact, Paul himself calls it a "mystery" (11:25). Some think "the fullness" refers to a specific number that only God knows, while others think it could refer to a great Gentile revival unlike the world has ever seen. But here's what we do know from Scripture:

2. **Read Matthew 24:14.** What will happen before the end will come?

3. **Read Revelation 7:9.** Who was accounted for in the great multitude?

While we don't know what "the fullness of the Gentiles" means, we do know that by the end, every nation will have been given access to the gospel.

A second mystery in this section is about the salvation of Israel. First, it's important to note that this is not referring to figurative Israel. The context of the previous chapters tells us this is not the spiritual "sons of Abraham," but the nation of Israel. Second, Paul said "all Israel will be saved" (11:26). There are many ideas on how this salvation of Israel will come about and its implications—but the fact remains that none of us knows for sure.

Despite these mysteries, one thing is clear, and this detail undergirds any mysteries or truths we don't yet fully understand: God has not given up on Israel.

**Review 11:28–32.**

4. What does 11:28 mean when Paul says, "As regards the gospel, they are enemies for your sake"? **(For a hint, look at 11:11.)**

Jewish people are not the enemy of Gentiles. Some were, at one time, enemies of the gospel, which opened the door to salvation for the Gentiles. But because God has chosen their forefathers, the Jews can rejoice that salvation is available to them.

★ 5. What does it say about God's character that His gifts and calling are irrevocable?

6. In 11:30–32, the word *mercy* appeared four times. What was it always in response to?

Every act or attitude of disobedience was met with mercy. We've learned a lot in the last couple of weeks about "the elect" and God's "choosing"— but notice that in each of these instances, God could have poured out His wrath to wipe the slate clean, destroying humanity. After all, Jews and Gentiles alike acted disobediently. But in all of this rebellion, He chose to have mercy on all who will believe.

It's no wonder this led Paul to his outpouring of praise.

**Review 11:33–36.**

This is another of Paul's doxologies in this letter.

7. Pop quiz! What does the word *doxology* mean? (Review the weekly challenge from last week if you need a reminder.)

Paul simply could not help himself. As he reflected on the mercies of God, he erupted in praise of his sovereign and holy Father.

★ 8. List all the things Paul praised God for in these verses. Based on something new you've learned recently, what would you add to Paul's praises?

Everything God revealed about Himself to Paul led him to praise. Even for Paul, this theology was difficult to comprehend, but instead of walking away from his calling or wringing his hands in despair, he glorified God!

What a wonderful example to us of what this sovereignty of God should ignite in our hearts! We simply cannot comprehend the vastness of God or the depths of His mercy toward us. He's our judge, but He's also our Savior. He's our refiner, but He's also our redeemer. He's our lawgiver, but He's also our counselor. And in all these things, He's where the joy is!

9. What stood out to you most in this week's study? Why?

10. What did you learn or relearn about God and His character this week?

# Corresponding Psalm & Prayer

 **READ PSALM 30**

1. What correlation do you see between Psalm 30 and this week's study?

2. What portions of this psalm stand out to you most?

3. Close by praying this prayer aloud:

*Father,*
     *You have lifted me up, given me help, and healed me! You give me grace and mercy. Because of You, my salvation is certain and*

*my hope is secure. I sing praise to You and give thanks to Your holy name. The glory is all Yours.*

*But even as I'm grateful that You redeemed my life from the pit, I fail to pray for others who remain there. My heart doesn't break for the lost as it should. And I haven't shared the good news about You as You've called me to do.*

*Instead of indifference about the lost, give me a longing for their salvation. Instead of apathy, give me a plan and an opportunity to share the truth about You. Instead of uneasiness, grant me a joyful determination to talk about the beauty of Your grace and mercy with people who don't yet know You.*

*Remind me that You alone have the power to save, and that I have the responsibility to share. Grant me obvious opportunities to talk about You, and give me the courage to do it! I surrender my life to You, Lord—every moment of my day, each decision I make, I yield my will and way to Your perfect will and way.*

*I love You too. Amen.*

# Rest, Catch Up, or Dig Deeper

## ✚ WEEKLY CHALLENGE

In Romans 10, Paul urged his audience to take the gospel to those who have never heard. What safer place to learn how to share the gospel than among Christian friends!

This week, spend time walking through a gospel outline* with another believer. The more you discuss the story of Jesus with a friend, the more comfortable you'll feel articulating it to someone new. After using this week to learn the outline, challenge yourself to share Jesus with someone before your study of Romans ends.

*If you need help, visit Dare2Share.org/Resources to find helpful resources and outlines for sharing the gospel.

# Romans 12

## DAILY BIBLE READING

Day 1: Romans 12:1–2

Day 2: Romans 12:3–8

Day 3: Romans 12:9–13

Day 4: Romans 12:14–18

Day 5: Romans 12:19–21

Day 6: Psalm 11

Day 7: Catch-Up Day

Corresponds to Day 344 of *The Bible Recap*.

## WEEKLY CHALLENGE

See page 225 for more information.

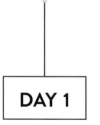

# Romans 12:1–2

 **READ ROMANS 12:1–2**

**Review 12:1.**

Paul spent the first eleven chapters of Romans ensuring his readers correctly understood the gospel and its implications. His last chapter ended with a reminder that all we have is a gift from God. Then he opened Romans 12 with our rightful response to God's good gifts; and he signaled this transition with the word *therefore*. We can't represent Jesus through our actions (and accurately point others to Him) if we don't first understand who He is and what He's done. Doing should always follow doctrine.

1. **Look up *doctrine* in a dictionary and write the definition below.**

Paul prompted his readers' response with the Greek word *parakaleō*. He wrote, "I appeal to you, brothers," or, as other translations read, "I urge you, brothers." While it may seem like Paul was presenting a strong command to the Romans, he wasn't. *Parakaleō* was one of the most gentle and considerate words Paul could have used to invite a response to his teaching. God isn't an unfeeling, militant commander looking for blind, rote obedience. He's attentive to the motivations of hearts (Psalm 51:16–17).

2. "Doing Christian things" (e.g., reading your Bible, going to church, serving, etc.) is an important part of your relationship with Christ. But sometimes those good and beautiful behaviors can be driven by motives that don't honor God such as pride, selfishness, or even shame. Ask God to reveal anything hidden about your motives so that you can better honor Him. Write down anything meaningful you discover.

Paul asked the Romans to respond to God's mercy. Like we've discussed, *mercy* is the withholding of deserved punishment, and *grace* means punishment is replaced with undeserved kindness or compassion. God most clearly evidenced His mercy to us through Christ's life, death on the cross, and resurrection (Titus 3:4–7).

Paul's next statement may seem shocking: "Present your bodies as a living sacrifice." To understand this, we need to look at two important phases of God's relationship with His people: the old covenant and the new covenant.

Under the old covenant, God required pure sacrifices and offerings. While their status as God's chosen people and God's love for them were unconditional, some of His promises did have conditions. And some of those conditions required priests and animal sacrifices.

Paul knew the Romans were familiar with the old covenant's sacrificial system, so he spoke their language to guide their response to God's mercy under the new covenant, which was ushered in with Christ.

Paul told the Romans to present their bodies as a *living* sacrifice. Their bodies were to be the "holy and acceptable" sacrifices to God. *Holy* means "set apart." So what were their bodies to be set apart from?

**Review 12:2.**

Paul urged the Romans to resist imitating the secular culture, entertainment, people, and belief systems in the world around them.

3. **Read 1 John 2:16 in the NIV.** Which of the following is not listed in John's description of the world?

  A. The lust of the flesh

  B. The lust of the eyes

  C. The pride of life

  D. The comforts of sleep

The Roman Christians' values and priorities should have set them apart from the world. Instead of attending activities like the gruesome gladiator games, Paul encouraged them to be transformed. Notice that Paul didn't encourage the Romans to transform or renew *themselves*. They weren't the active agent in that process. He encouraged them to allow God to transform them by the renewal of their minds. So how did this transforming and renewing take place?

4. **Look up the word *renewal* (12:2) in a Greek lexicon. Now look up the only other time in Scripture where this word is used and write the verse reference below.** Who is the active agent mentioned in that verse (the one responsible for the renewal process)?

As we discussed in Romans 8, sanctification is the process by which the Spirit works in us to make us look more like Jesus. *That's* the will of God—that we'd look like Jesus (1 Thessalonians 4:3). Paul's challenge to the Roman Christians was that they fully and intentionally submit to the work of the Spirit, the one who renews their minds. He does the doing!

In addition to submission, the Roman Christians' role in this process was to "test" their thoughts to see if they lined up with the truths of God. He prompted them to continuously evaluate what they were thinking about. This applies to us today too.

★ 5. What do you spend most of your time thinking about? Are your thoughts helping you become more like Christ?

If you're unsure whether your actions, choices, or thoughts honor God, you have a great opportunity to exercise discernment and wisdom. This begins with comparing (or testing) your ideologies, motives, or actions with God's Word and character. God's will always aligns with His Word and His way.

For areas that may be unclear or that aren't explicitly addressed in Scripture, pray for increased sensitivity to the Spirit's leadership and ask for wisdom from those around you who know and love God. (As an added bonus, this is also a great opportunity to be truly known in your church or Chrisitan community.)

6. Do you ever struggle to course correct when you realize the path you're on doesn't align with God's will? Explain. Who could you ask for help? Be specific.

# Romans 12:3–8

## ✝ READ ROMANS 12:3-8

There are three important keys to understanding spiritual gifts. First, spiritual gifts are different from natural gifts. Both types of gifts are given by God for His glory, but spiritual gifts are assigned only to God's kids to benefit the church (1 Corinthians 12:7; 1 Peter 4:11). It's helpful to view spiritual gifts as ways to serve the body of Christ; they are outward focused.

Second, because the lists vary each time we see them in Scripture (Exodus 31:1–6; Romans 12:6–8; 1 Corinthians 12:8–28; Ephesians 4:11; 1 Peter 4:9–11), they don't appear to be all-inclusive; instead, they seem to expand and adapt to fill the present needs of the body. This also means your gifts may not be a lifelong assignment; they may change as the needs within the body change. They appear to be situationally determined.

Third, while every believer will receive a gift, the same gift may look different in the life of each person who has it, and some people may receive multiple gifts and ways to serve the body. Paul even indicates that if you are eager to serve in multiple ways, you can ask God to grant you a gift you don't already have (1 Corinthians 12:31); however, the answer to that prayer—whether yes, no, or wait—remains up to the Giver, of course.

**Review 12:3.**

When Paul wrote, "For by the grace given to me . . ." he was reminding his Roman audience that his role as an apostle was given to him by God. Just as he hadn't earned his title on his own, the Roman Christians hadn't earned their gifts either. He had a humble posture.

205

1. It's been said that "humility isn't thinking less of yourself—it's thinking of yourself less." Or in other words, it's having an external focus, thinking of others more. Review the first paragraph from today's study, then fill in the blanks below.

My spiritual gifts are for _____ glory.

My spiritual gifts are for _____ _____ benefit.

Paul wanted the Romans to understand their gifts correctly. By writing, "Think with sober judgment, each according to the measure of faith that God has assigned," he was basically saying, *"Hey, Romans, before you open a present, look at the card! Make sure you know who gave it to you. Then you can correctly understand what you've been given and why."*

When believers realize the gifts we've received look different from our peers', we may be tempted to compare. This is a trap! It puts the focus back on the self. We can avoid that trap when we humbly remember the truth: God gave all of us at least one critically useful gift, and we need one another. Everyone's gift is vital and valuable.

**Review 12:4–5.**

The church isn't a bunch of individuals doing their own thing for Jesus, separated from other believers. Jesus made Christianity a team sport. We're only able to be unified as one body (the church) because we're first unified in Christ, who is the head of the body.

2. Paul describes this team effort by comparing it to various body parts working together as one collective organism. **Read 1 Corinthians 12:14–31 and list all the body parts he named.**

**Review 12:6–8.**

★ 3. **Read 1 Peter 4:10 and summarize it in your own words.**

After ensuring the Romans understood who their gifts came from and what they were for, Paul encouraged them to use their gifts and to do so joyfully. What good is a new basketball if it never gets inflated and used by the team?

4. **Consult a Bible dictionary and briefly define the terms below.**

| Gift | Description |
|---|---|
| Prophecy | Scholars have differing views on this gift. Some think it no longer exists. Others believe it's the act of declaring the already-revealed Word of God in a strengthening, encouraging, and comforting way (1 Corinthians 14:3). And others believe it is a supernatural discernment in a particular situation or event. This gift also has a unique aspect: prophecy came in "proportion to faith," meaning the degree to which a person faithfully followed Jesus would determine how seriously others took his or her prophetic words. |
| Service | |

| Gift | Description |
|---|---|
| Teaching | Teaching is the ability to explain and effectively communicate the truth of the Bible to others without any formal training (though a person's preparation before teaching may also utilize the gift). Although you could study to become a teacher, the gift of teaching, like all gifts, can't be taught. A person gifted in teaching can explain the gist, context, and application of Scripture in a more impactful way than someone who doesn't have the gift. |
| Exhortation | |
| Giving ("the one who contributes") | |
| Leadership | |
| Mercy | |

You may be thinking, *But what if I don't know what my gift is?* Discovering your gift(s) is a normal part of the Christian life. If you aren't sure what your gifts are, ask your local church how your presence there has been beneficial to the body. If you haven't been using your gifts (or are still discovering them), ask your local church if there are any needs you can help meet. Not only will the Spirit reveal your gift(s) to you, but others will see it in you and affirm it. And remember, your spiritual gift(s) might not align with your natural talents or passions; God might be opening new doors for you to serve that you've never even thought about before!

★ 5. If you know your current spiritual gifts, what are they? If you don't know, what's your best next step?

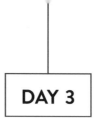

# Romans 12:9–13

## ✝ READ ROMANS 12:9–13

Yesterday we learned that spiritual gifts are for God's glory and to build up the church. In short, spiritual gifts are for the benefit of others. Continuing with this theme, Paul's words to the Romans in today's section are others-focused: How should believers treat one another?

**Review 12:9.**

Before Paul called the Romans to love, he described love. Christian love shouldn't be hypocritical. It should be genuine and honest.

1. **Using a Greek lexicon, look up the word used for *love* in 12:9. What does it mean?**

There are multiple biblical words for love. *Agape* refers to the love God has for His people. It's demonstrated through His Son's life, death, resurrection, and ascension—it's a godly love. It's unconditional, selfless, and pure. This is the type of love Christians should be marked by (1 John 4:19). And just like our God, who is love, is opposed to evil, Paul pointed out that the Roman believers should be too (John 1:5; 1 John 4:8; Ephesians 6:13).

**Review 12:10–13.**

*Philia* love marked friendships. *Storge* love marked the love shared between family members. But in Romans 12:10, Paul smashed them together and used the word *philostorgos* when he wrote, "Love one another with brotherly affection." It's like Paul was saying the love shared between believers should emulate the familiarity or safety of family and the longevity or trust present in a strong friendship.

2. Think about your closest friend or a favorite family member. List two memories you share, two of their positive traits, and two reasons why you respect them. In other words, why do you give them your time?

Paul explained that the love believers share should be accompanied by honor. The love that marks Christians should resemble the type of love you'd express to someone you've known your entire life, and it should include the type of honor that says they're worthy of being served by you. Honor demonstrates value. When we serve others, we affirm they have value, because they're made in the image of the one true God, who is love.

★ 3. This is the only place in the entire Bible where the Greek word for *outdo* (12:10) is used. **Look it up in a Greek lexicon and summarize its meaning in your own words.**

Christians shouldn't be lazy when serving Christ or one another. They should be eager to serve. Oftentimes, it's easier for a new Christian to be zealous because everything's new and exciting. Likewise, after attending a retreat or conference, you may ride a "spiritual high." We're eager to respond when we've had an impactful spiritual experience. The downside to this is that when we don't experience a spiritual high, finding motivation (or zeal) can be difficult. And if you've been walking with Jesus for many years, it may be tempting to view your faith as a responsibility rather than a gift. Paul has some challenging words for us.

4. Paul presented three instructions in 12:11. Pay careful attention to the order. Write Paul's instructions below.

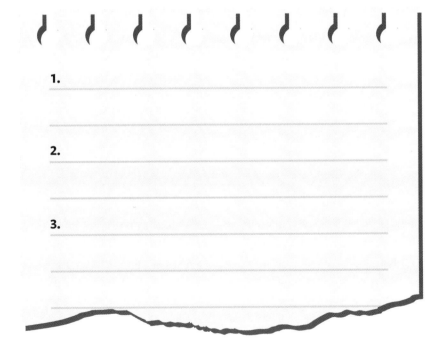

1.

2.

3.

Remember back in 12:2 when Paul wrote that the Romans were to be transformed and renewed instead of transforming and renewing themselves? Here, in the middle of 12:11, Paul reminds us again of how that happens by sandwiching the main ingredient. True transformation and zeal are only possible when a person is sensitive and surrendered to the Spirit's work in their life.

5. Knowing that, go back and circle the main ingredient on the list above.

The Spirit empowers the action. If you aren't surrendered to the Spirit, it's like you're trying to drive a car while the gas tank is on empty. Being fervent in spirit means consistently looking to the Spirit for leadership, direction, wisdom, the pace of life, power over temptation, comfort, encouragement, strength, peace, and more! Understanding the Spirit's role is the secret to the behaviors and attitudes Paul encouraged throughout the rest of his letter to the Roman Christians.

★ 6. After highlighting the Spirit's role, Paul provided five examples of service in 12:12–13. Underline the behavior where you find yourself relying on the Spirit the most. Circle the behavior where you rely on the Spirit the least. Explain.

> Rejoicing in Christ's future coming
>
> Patience when experiencing a trial
>
> Persistent prayer
>
> Generosity
>
> Hospitality

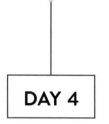

# Romans 12:14–18

 **READ ROMANS 12:14–18**

In today's text, Paul shared principles with the Roman Christians that were true not only for them, but for all believers.

**Review 12:14.**

While Paul's words are applicable today, the Roman church was still young and figuring out how everyone should act. The new covenant truths we learned about in Romans 12:2 were there to guide their way of life.

1. Pop quiz! Do you remember the definition of *mercy*? Do your best to write it from memory below. Then go back to Day 3 of Week 7 to check your work.

Payback should never be the way of Christians. Paul made it clear that even if the Romans were persecuted, they should bless those who mistreated them. Blessing involves both wanting God's best for people and praying for them.

★ 2. When someone wrongs you, are you tempted to retaliate, whether in action or thought? Explain.

**Review 12:15.**

Paul called the Romans to celebrate with those who celebrate and grieve with those who grieve. He didn't say, "Advise those who grieve"; in fact, that's the opposite of his instruction. When we come alongside a friend who's grieving, we should meet them in their pain. Sit with them. Cry with them. Pray with them. Resist the urge to provide an answer or to try to end their tears. Sometimes, all a grieving person needs is the presence of a faithful friend.

★ 3. How does the world suggest you respond to those who are grieving? Do your responses typically look more like the world's or more like Paul's instructions to the Romans? Give an example.

**Review 12:16.**

Christian unity transcends socioeconomic levels. Feelings of superiority weren't (and aren't) warranted or appropriate for anyone who had been rescued and washed clean by the blood of Jesus.

In Christ, we're all sinners who needed and still need the Savior. And we're part of the same family—the unity and harmony that mark believers combat all socioeconomic biases and prejudices held by God's people before meeting Christ. In Him, we are one. This work of unity is a work of the Spirit. So it's important we remember that all our responses to Christ require our surrender to the empowering movement of His Spirit.

4. In 12:16, what type of attitude did Paul prohibit? Describe this attitude in your own words. What did Paul encourage?

Paul encouraged the Romans to go above and beyond to serve others, even when it felt unfair, rather than repay evil for evil. In Paul's day, a Roman soldier could approach a civilian and say, "Pick up my stuff," demanding they carry their gear (on foot) for one mile. But Jesus, in Matthew 5:41, called them to an even higher standard: He told them to go *two* miles instead.

**Review 12:17–18.**

This "go the extra mile" rule could be implemented only in response to someone else's request; similarly, here Paul was giving reactive instruction to the Romans. (Don't worry, he'll give proactive instruction later; we'll see this when we study 14:19.) Paul was focusing on how the Romans should respond to injustice, unkindness, and even evil. The Romans couldn't control how others responded, acted, or spoke, but they *were* in control of their own responses.

It's worth noting that Paul wasn't saying to let others walk all over you. And he definitely wasn't saying to take the blame for something you didn't do. Paul was telling the Romans to respond to others by taking the lead in the pursuit of peace as much as they possibly could.

5. When it comes to living peaceably, are there any relationships or situations you need to take the lead in? Write a prayer asking the Spirit to help you.

# Romans 12:19–21

 **READ ROMANS 12:19–21**

**Review 12:19.**

Paul called the Romans "beloved." This implied they were loved and esteemed. It's like Paul was saying, *"I'm about to give you a high standard, but it's fitting for you."* As Christ loved the Roman believers and wanted what was best for them, so did Paul. He didn't want them to get carried away seeking payback. Revenge always reeks of a lack of trust in God.

Paul reminded the Romans that God could be trusted to right any wrongs they'd encountered. While believers have a responsibility to defend the weak, pursue justice, and live wisely, it's not our job to retaliate when we're attacked (Isaiah 1:17; Proverbs 22:3). The temptation to respond incorrectly vanishes when we remember God's wrath.

★ 1. Flip back to Week 1, Day 3 (page 24). What did you learn about the wrath of God? Write the definition below.

Recognizing his Roman audience was familiar with the Torah, Paul referenced Deuteronomy 32:35 when he said, "Vengeance is mine, I will repay, says the Lord." This confidence-boosting one-liner came from a prophetic sermon Moses gave, and it called to mind several hundred years of fulfilled history:

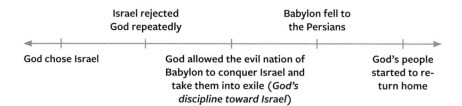

Even though God used Babylon to discipline Israel, he didn't let their unrighteousness go unpunished. He judged Babylon too. Vengeance is always God's, and Paul's Roman audience knew this historical fact. It was tried and true.

2. Identify God's vengeance toward Babylon by circling it on the timeline above.

**Review 12:20.**

In the Old Testament, "burning coals" represented punishment, and they were often described as a result of God's righteous judgment. But some ancient cultures had a tradition of carrying a pan of burning coals over their head as a symbol of sorrow and repentance. So because God is the only righteous judge (as Paul proved in previous chapters), and because vengeance belongs to Him alone, how were the Romans heaping burning coals on the heads of their enemies? Simply put, by being kind. They were to let their love and way of life be uncomfortable to those who practiced evil.

3. Match the following scenarios with the reactions Paul encouraged.

| | |
|---|---|
| Your enemy is hungry | Give him something to drink |
| Your enemy is thirsty | Metaphorically heap burning coals on your enemy |
| By providing food and drink | Feed him |

**Review 12:21.**

Here, Paul said, "Do not be overcome by evil." Given the context, it's clear he didn't mean *"Don't let your enemy win"*; instead, he's essentially saying, *"Don't give in to your temptation to get payback or revenge."* He was referring to every believer's battle against the evil (or sin) that tries to rise up within us. We should be more focused on beating *our* evil tendencies (i.e., the flesh), not someone else's.

For modern believers, this means our time isn't best spent getting more aggressive on social media. When our neighbors fly a flag we consider wicked, this verse isn't suggesting that the solution is to fly a *bigger* flag for our own cause.

★ 4. When are you most tempted to fight someone else's "evil" rather than the sin that lives in you?

The Romans had to be watchful not to let their allegiance to God alienate them from the world they were intended to reach with the gospel. Rather, through their allegiance to Christ and the power of the Spirit, they could respond to the people who didn't know Jesus in a way that rightly represented Him and His kingdom. They could patiently work to be others-focused, to put the flesh to death, and to point to the beauty of God and His kingdom. How brightly His love shines in the midst of the darkness! He's where the joy is!

5. What stood out to you most in this week's study? Why?

6. What did you learn or relearn about God and His character this week?

# Corresponding Psalm & Prayer

 **READ PSALM 11**

1. What correlation do you see between Psalm 11 and this week's study?

2. What portions of this psalm stand out to you most?

3. Close by praying this prayer aloud:

*Father,*
   *You are in Your holy temple, yet You are my ever-present ref-
uge. Your throne is in heaven, yet You are always near. You are the*

*righteous judge, and You alone will rain coals on the wicked. I can rest in Your grace, because Your Word says the righteous will behold Your face. And because You have made me righteous, one day I will behold Your face!*

*Even as I've declared Your righteousness, I've sought my own revenge for wrongs done to me. Forgive me and fill my heart with confidence in Your timing to judge the wicked. Give me the desire and ability to treat them kindly.*

*I've opened the gifts You've given me and been dismissive of them. I've seen the gifts You've given others and been envious of them. And I repent. Forgive me and fill my heart with gratitude. My love for You and for my fellow believers has been conditional, selfish, and tainted. Forgive me and fill my heart with* philostorgos, *brotherly love.*

*You call me to be transformed, and You transform me. You are working to renew my mind! As You transform me and renew my mind, I surrender my life to You, Lord—every moment of my day, each decision I make, I yield my will and way to Your perfect will and way.*

*I love You too. Amen.*

# Rest, Catch Up, or Dig Deeper

## ✝ WEEKLY CHALLENGE

Read through the marks of a true Christian listed in Romans 12:9–21. Is the Spirit prompting you in any of these areas? Pray and ask Him how you can grow in it. Which of these ways of loving others and dying to self can you apply this week? Embrace the joy God is inviting you into as you pursue genuine love!

# Romans 13–14

┌─ **Scripture to Memorize** ─┐

But if Christ is in you, although the body is dead because of sin, the Spirit is life because of righteousness.

Romans 8:10

## DAILY BIBLE READING

Day 1: Romans 13:1–7

Day 2: Romans 13:8–14

Day 3: Romans 14:1–12

Day 4: Romans 14:13–19

Day 5: Romans 14:20–23

Day 6: Psalm 116

Day 7: Catch-Up Day

Corresponds to Days 344 and 345 of *The Bible Recap.*

## WEEKLY CHALLENGE

See page 254 for more information.

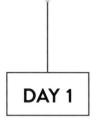

# Romans 13:1–7

 **READ ROMANS 13:1-7**

Romans 12 ended with Paul urging the Romans Christians not to seek revenge because vengeance belongs to the Lord, and He can be trusted. Here, Paul transitioned to discussing submission to earthly authorities—things such as the law of the land, governments, and the rulers who were in authority over his audience. This, too, requires trust in God.

There's connective tissue between today's chapter and the last one. In today's text, we see that earthly authorities do have the authority to enact punishments. This is the case because they are, in fact, the authorities God has appointed.

**Review 13:1.**

Paul said, "Let every person be subject to the governing authorities." This doesn't leave anyone out.

1. According to 13:1, what are the only two authorities that exist?

This can be a challenging teaching to take in initially. When you think of authorities, perhaps a local official like a judge or a governor comes to mind. Maybe you think of a president or a king or even a violent dictator, and you wonder how that fits into this equation.

★ 2. Do you find it comforting that Paul said God has appointed the authorities in our lives? Or do you find it challenging or disturbing? Describe.

This teaching would have been no less challenging (and, in fact, probably more so) to the Romans in Paul's day. Many of them lived under the rule of the same Roman leaders that kicked them out of the city for being Jewish (Acts 18:2), fed Christians to the wild animals in the Colosseum, and—during the emperor Nero's time—lit them on fire as human torches at garden parties. Submission to authority was no small request for the Roman Christians.*

**Review 13:2–4.**

Perhaps 13:2 made you wonder if revolutions are a sin. That's a weighty question. Paul was telling his Roman audience that because governments have authority from God, they were obliged to obey them. But this is an important place to remember that we take in the full counsel of God. Elsewhere in Scripture (Acts 5:29, for example) obedience to God is emphasized over obedience to man. In both instances, the common thread is trusting God's authority.

   Authorities are God's servants for our good. This is not a new idea. In Romans 8, we learned that God works all things together for the good of believers—even when we can't see or understand it. Throughout Scripture, He tells us He's sovereign over every ruler and authority.

---

*It's worth noting that Nero was also the emperor when Paul was executed.

3. **Look up the following verses and summarize them in your own words.**

Proverbs 21:1

Daniel 2:21

Matthew 28:18

Let's take a quick look at the story of Jesus's birth and see how it proves this truth.

4. What name do you find in Luke 2:1? What did he do?

Caesar Augustus probably thought this census was working for his own purposes and plans. But God was sovereign over this move from the start. How do we know this? An Old Testament prophecy reveals a bit more about what was happening in this story.

5. What city is mentioned in Micah 5:2?

The prophet Micah foretold that Jesus would be born in Bethlehem—more than seven hundred years before it happened. Joseph and Mary traveled there because they were required to do so for the census, and thus, that's where Jesus was born. Caesar Augustus had no desire to help fulfill a prophecy of a promised savior for the Jews, who were Caesar's subjects. But God was sovereign over the plans Caesar thought were his own.

**Review 13:5–7.**

Paul followed these godly principles with specific guidelines. He was confronting the practice of zealous Jews of the time who refused to pay taxes in order to "have no king but God." But—and this one may resonate more with us as modern readers—he was also addressing any thoughts of his Roman audience that because they were set apart and obedient to God, they didn't have to follow earthly rules anymore.

Paul was setting them straight. He was establishing not that Christians should be passable citizens, but should, in fact, endeavor to be *excellent* citizens. He was essentially saying, *"Pay your taxes. Pay your parking tickets. Be blessings to your state. Pray for them."* That directive applies even in unexpected places.

★ 6. How did God tell the Jews in exile to behave in Jeremiah 29:4–7? What does God specifically say about the welfare of the city in 29:7? Are there any ways this could apply to your life?

7. Write a prayer for your leaders, your nation, your community.

# Romans 13:8–14

 **READ ROMANS 13:8-14**

**Review 13:8–9.**

Some take the words of 13:8, "Owe no one anything," as a scriptural command to never borrow money. However, in the greater context of Scripture, we see that borrowing and lending were permitted, even by Jesus.

1. **Look up Matthew 5:42 and Proverbs 22:7.** Summarize what you find about borrowing and lending.

Scripture does warn of the pitfalls that can accompany borrowing and lending, but what Paul was telling the Roman Christians in 13:8 was that our debt to love one another is never finished or paid. We can pay our debts and act as fiscally responsible members of society. But when it comes to love, that's something we're commanded to continually do—to keep doing it even when it's hard, even when we feel like we've already given *quite enough, thank you*. Paul said all the other commandments are summed up in this word.

2. What is that "word"?

It's important to note that Paul didn't tell the Romans to throw all the other commandments out and replace them with this one; he said many of the commandments could be *summed up* in it.

3. In the table below, next to each commandment, write how you think loving your neighbor as yourself might compel you to obey it. The first one is filled in for you.

| | |
|---|---|
| **You shall not commit adultery.** | Loving my neighbor as myself would compel me to consider my neighbor above myself and my own sexual desires, to care more about how the adultery would affect others than about myself. |
| **You shall not murder.** | |
| **You shall not steal.** | |
| **You shall not covet.** | |

★ 4. What does the phrase *as yourself* mean? What might that look like in your own life when practically applied?

**Review 13:10.**

In Matthew 22:36–40, Jesus said all the Law and Prophets hang on these two commandments: (1) Love the Lord your God with all your heart and with all your soul and with all your mind, and (2) love your neighbor as yourself. It's possible to do religious things and neglect love, but the point made here is this: Love is actually the *fulfilling* of the law.

**Review 13:11–14.**

Paul gave six actions that point to the truth that love is an active calling—and reflective of the condition of our own hearts, not the "lovability" of others.

5. From 13:11–14, list the six actions, and, in parenthesis, add what they correspond to. The first one is done for you.

A. Wake (from sleep)

B.

C.

D.

E.

F.

In this passage, Paul clarified to the Romans that their personal pursuit of holiness directly correlated to their ability to love others well. If we aren't rightly responding to God and His commands, we'll be unable to rightly love others. It begins with God.

★ 6. Briefly describe a situation where you recognized that your relationship with God impacts your ability to love others.

A command like "Love your neighbor . . . *forever*" can feel exhausting. But we know the commands we live out as Christians aren't done in our own strength—it's the power of God working through us (Philippians 2:13). We can do all things through Christ who strengthens us (Philippians 4:13)

Paul said time is short. Lethargy—or spiritual sleepwalking—is a common temptation for Christians. Satan wants to trick us into thinking what we do doesn't matter, or that it only matters for *us*, or that there's plenty of time for doing the work of God later. But when Paul said, "The day is at hand," he was referring to the return of Jesus. Paul was saying (as Jesus did in Revelation 22:12) that Jesus is coming back soon.

7. Which of the following are the specific works of darkness Paul said to cast off in 13:12–13?

    A. orgies and drunkenness

    B. sexual immorality and sensuality

    C. quarreling and jealousy

    D. eating meat sacrificed to idols

    E. all but D

Do you know what "armor of light" means? We aren't reading a super-hero novel, so don't fly past this phrase thinking it's just a collection of cool-sounding words or something that exists only in a fairy tale. If God's Word says we can put on the armor of light, then the armor of light is something we have access to and can put on.

8. **Using your favorite Bible study tools, research "armor of light" (13:12).** Write what you find. Ask God to help you accept His offer and put it on!

The phrase "make no provision for the flesh" in 13:14 doesn't refer to the physical needs of the flesh, like food, water, or shelter. *Flesh* here refers to sin and its desires. Paul told the Romans to approach all these things actively: Love is active, avoiding sin is active, putting on the Lord Jesus Christ is active. And—praise God—Hebrews 4:12 tells us that even the words you read in this passage of Scripture moments ago are active and capable of piercing the very soul!

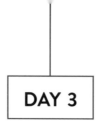

DAY 3

# Romans 14:1–12

 **READ ROMANS 14:1-12**

Today's study begins with an imperative to welcome the one who's weak in faith. Before making assumptions about what Paul meant by "weak" (14:1), let's take a look at how he elaborated on his description.

**Review 14:1–4.**

1. In 14:2 below, circle the part of the verse that refers to the "strong" person, and circle the part that refers to the "weak" person. Label each accordingly.

> "One person believes he may eat anything, while the weak person eats only vegetables."

What's going on here? Was Paul a foodie? Was he obsessed with diets? Was he really talking about vegetables, or was he speaking metaphorically? The answer to that last question is *both*.

On the one hand, Paul was addressing a specific issue in the church. The Jewish Christians were concerned about eating meat that (1) violated Mosaic law, (2) violated the many additional restrictions the Jewish leaders had added to the Mosaic law, or (3) had been offered as a sacrifice to other gods, as was common in this Roman culture. So Paul wasn't making fun of vegetarians here. He was specifically addressing Jewish Christians who thought of themselves as the stronger, more morally upright ones in the church because they abstained from more foods than their Gentile fellow believers.

It's easy to assume the "weaker" believers were the ones who were "looser" with their restrictions, whereas the "stronger" believers further along in their faith were more restrictive. But Paul said the stricter one was the weaker one. The one who had the maturity to live in freedom but also knew when to rein it in had more strength.

However, it's important to note that there's a difference between weak and rebellious. Paul was *not* saying the "stronger" believers were free to be sinful or selfish.

2. What were the Romans told not to quarrel over in 14:1?

There are absolutes in our faith—gospel issues that are not up for debate, such as the deity of Jesus and salvation by grace alone, through faith alone, in Christ alone.* But in this passage, Paul was addressing *opinions*, not sin. The only sin being discussed in this passage was human judgment. Some opinions might even be Bible-based or holiness-driven. But when the Bible doesn't make something an absolute, neither can we.

★ 3. Have you witnessed—or been a part of—disagreements over opinions within the church? How did those disagreements affect the relationships of the people involved?

*For more information about the distinctions between absolutes, convictions, opinions, and questions, visit MyDGroup.org/beliefs.

Paul specifically told the Romans not to judge, because we all have our "own master." Was he saying we have different gods? Or that we are our own masters? To use one of Paul's favorite phrases, *not at all!* Paul was saying our relationship with God is a personal one. This doesn't give us an excuse to sin. He wasn't telling the Romans that God lets some people sin and not others. God's law is perfect and true in every corner of the universe. Paul was talking about maturity and how God tugs at each of our hearts over different issues at different times. Humility is key to understanding the heart of this message.

**Review 14:5–9.**

Here, Paul used a new example: the differing preferences these church members had for observing special days in the calendar. This variety of examples helps us see he wasn't necessarily trying to address specific issues; instead, it seems he was addressing the principle. The command here wasn't to eliminate differences, but to rise above them.

4. True or false: When Paul said "each one should be fully convinced in his own mind," he was saying, *"Follow your truth! Do what's right for you!"*

Paul has already been very clear in other passages as to the immutable commands God gives us. And he's already been clear in his ministry about going the extra mile, even sacrificing our own comfort, to avoid being a stumbling block to others. He wasn't implying that whatever we feel is permissible *is* permissible. He was addressing the temptation to judge one another's preferences, and he was saying, *"Don't do it."*

5. In 14:8–9, how does Christ's authority as Lord over life and death reinforce Paul's teaching? **(Use your favorite Bible study tools for help if needed.)**

**Review 14:10–12.**

6. For what reason do we not pass judgment on one another?

★ 7. The "judgment seat of God" (14:10) is also known as the "bema seat." **Do a web search for this term and note what you find.** Is this what you expected? Why or why not?

This is not the judgment seat all humanity will stand before. Paul was addressing believers here, and this is a judgment seat all *believers* will stand before in regard to their positions and rewards in the kingdom. Paul was ending this passage saying, *"Don't quarrel. Save it for God at the bema seat."*

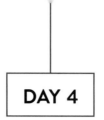

# Romans 14:13–19

## ✝ READ ROMANS 14:13-19

You've likely seen or heard someone taking a Bible verse out of context, disregarding the full counsel of the Word of God—or perhaps you've even been guilty of this yourself. Paul doesn't want us to forget that this is one long letter filled with cause and effect, motive and result—that's why he's a big "therefore" guy. His letter has continuity—it's a detailed, nuanced teaching, woven together by a contextual thread.

So when Paul discussed judgment in this section, he wasn't laying out an isolated directive to never judge. He was reminding the Romans of the heart behind all these points: to bless one another in our living, and to not worry about whether others are blessing us, because we'll all be judged by God.

1. In your own words, summarize what each verse says (or demonstrates) about judging.

John 7:24

Romans 15:14

2 Timothy 4:2

James 4:11–12

**Review 14:13–15.**

In yesterday's study, we discussed the important distinction between absolutes and opinions in our faith. Scripture says rebuke or admonishment is only to be done over absolutes—not over opinions that Scripture itself is not clear about.

★ 2. Can you think of a time when judgment was shared with you in a way that modeled how Scripture tells us to judge and was ultimately a blessing to you? If so, describe.

When Paul said not to put a stumbling block in the way of a brother, he was warning against two extremes: beating one another down with legalism, and inconsiderately using our personal liberty in a way that induces others to sin.

To understand what Paul referred to when he mentioned unclean things, let's take a quick trip to Joppa, where the apostle Peter had a vision on a roof in the book of Acts.

3. **Read Acts 10:9–16.** Write what you find in Acts 10:15.

In 14:14, Paul addressed the huge shift God signaled to Peter in this vision. Until after the time of Christ's resurrection, Jews had lived under Mosaic law that prohibited the eating of certain animals. This vision was God's invitation to freedom from that directive. And though Peter shared this vision exuberantly with early church leadership, Paul was addressing the tendency among Jewish Christians to hold on to the cleanliness laws.

4. According to Acts 10:17–33, what happened as a result of this vision?

When the Gentiles heard the good news, the heart of that change wasn't unholiness, but unity, togetherness! Gentiles and Jews were sitting together at tables and communing in one another's homes—a shocking sight for both groups of people.

**Review 14:16–17.**

5. Which of the following do you think is meant by 14:16?

    A. Don't live in such a way that your use of personal liberty could become something that could *rightly* be spoken of as evil.

    B. If someone thinks something is good, but you think it's evil, your best approach is to post about it on social media or send a harshly worded email.

    C. Your focus and attention should be on the behavior of others.

    D. You should pluck the speck out of other people's eyes before addressing your log (Matthew 7:3–5).

6. True or false: There won't be food in eternity.

Great news: We serve a God who loves feasts. All of Scripture culminates with a prophecy of a dinner party better than anything we could imagine (Revelation 19:6–9). It's called the marriage supper of the Lamb, and all believers are included. Our God is not a God who doesn't care about the beauty of eating and drinking—He invented it, and He did it all the time when He was on earth. Jesus loved grabbing dinner with people! So what does 14:17 mean?

Paul was making the point that the kingdom of God is so much more than just the physical pleasures we have on this earth—and it certainly isn't about the watchdogging of one another's physical pleasures.

**Review 14:18–19.**

Heeding the wisdom of 14:18 might not mean every human in the room will give you the thumbs-up you're looking for. But it's a patient, mature exhortation, essentially saying, *"Live this way, and, ultimately, the overarching banner over your life will be one of approval by God and man."* It's also a call to action. *Pursue* here is not a passive word—it's an active word, compelling us to chase peace, to hunt it down.

★ 7. What do you think pursuing peace looks like in practice? List some examples of how you could pursue it in your own life.

# Romans 14:20–23

 READ ROMANS 14:20-23

Today's passage harkens back to what Paul said in 14:17. The kingdom of God is a matter of something so much better than eating and drinking.

**Review 14:20–21.**

Here, Paul was basically saying, *"Don't care more about the contents of your cup than the work God is doing in a fellow believer's life."*

Paul continually told the Romans to make choices that would help one another grow closer to Christ instead of hindering that growth. Paul's original audience would've been thinking about adhering to the Mosaic law. But today, it's tempting to take these verses and apply them in a legalistic sense, creating our own new set of rules. Paul reiterated that it's not about legalistically creating a list of rules so everyone can err on the side of perfection.

★ 1. Can you think of a situation where you were inclined to add rules to God's Word, maybe even out of what felt like good intentions? If so, describe.

Paul was clear that legalism can be as much of a stumbling block as liberty. That theme was the primary reason the early church held the Jerusalem Council in AD 50. Uncertainty over what was required of non-Jewish (Gentile) converts had been causing no small amount of disunity and drama in the formative days of the church. So a council of leaders, including Paul, gathered in Jerusalem to determine what behaviors were required and forbidden.

Ultimately, they decided to lay "no greater burden" on Gentile believers than four specific requirements.

**2. According to Acts 15:29, what were they called to abstain from? Circle all that are correct.**

| | |
|---|---|
| What has been sacrificed to idols | Blood |
| What has been strangled | Sexual immorality |
| Bread | |

The heart behind the council's decision was unity among Christ-followers. These requirements were *not* laid out as a means of salvation for the Gentile converts; their salvation was from Christ—just as it was for the Jewish converts to Christianity. These four requirements were about unifying a new melting pot of a church made up of both Jews and Gentiles, who, prior to this time, did not eat meals together. The reason they didn't sit at meals together was directly related to the list above, per the ceremonial laws God had given the Jews some 1,400 years earlier in Leviticus 17–18.

It's worth noting that we're seeing God work on hearts from both sides here. On the one hand, Paul was telling his Jewish brothers and sisters to lay down the restrictions God had freed them from for the sake of unity. And at the Jerusalem Council, Gentile Christians were asked to lay down some of their freedoms for the sake of that same unity.

**3. What was the Gentile Christians' response to this news in Acts 15:31?**

4. In Romans 14:21, which word comes first, *good* or *not*? What difference does that make?

Paul didn't say, "It is not good to . . ." He said, "It is good not to." He wasn't telling his Roman audience about something that was bad to do—he was telling them something that was good to do. He wasn't calling them all to be vegetarians; he was basically saying, *"It's good to care more about the person sitting beside you at the table than your pork loin and cabernet."*

**Review 14:22–23.**

Paul's words in 14:22 are often taken out of context by people who prefer to keep their faith on the down-low. But that certainly can't be what he meant—after all, Paul had already suffered immensely for sharing the gospel. His faith was so public that he was repeatedly imprisoned for it!

5. **Look up the word *keep* (14:22) in a Greek lexicon.** How does this definition help us know that Paul wasn't saying faith is a private matter?

Paul was essentially saying, *"If you're strong enough to live in certain liberties, use that same strength to pursue unity by abstaining from or not flaunting your liberties."* The person who doesn't condemn himself by prioritizing his liberties over his faith is happy and blessed. That person can trust that everything God has for him far exceeds any temporary delights.

★ 6. Can you think of a time when you traded something you thought made you happy for something so much better that you found in walking closely with God?

True happiness—being blessed—is only found in God. When we die to ourselves in order to follow Him, we find out that He's where the joy is!

7. What stood out to you most in this week's study? Why?

8. What did you learn or relearn about God and His character this week?

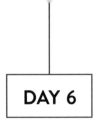

# Corresponding Psalm & Prayer

### ✝ READ PSALM 116

1. What correlation do you see between Psalm 116 and this week's study?

2. What portions of this psalm stand out to you most?

3. Close by praying this prayer aloud:

*Father,*
    *You have heard my voice and turned Your ear to me. I cried out in weakness and You gave me Your strength. I called for help and*

*You delivered me. I begged for mercy and You gave it. You have dealt bountifully with me and I praise You!*

*You are sovereign over all authorities in heaven and on earth. But I've failed to honor Your authority by failing to submit to the leaders You've put in place. And I've failed to respect and honor those in authority over me, with my words and with my thoughts. You are merciful, but in my legalism and licentiousness I have failed to honor Your mercy. I've been too strict with others, insisting that any of their convictions and opinions that don't match my own are sin. And at the same time, I've insisted on a right to my own liberties; sometimes even at the expense of causing my brothers and sisters to stumble and sin. And I repent.*

*Grant me a humble heart for unity. Grant me a willingness to submit, surrender, and obey. May my obedience bring You honor. May my words and actions teach others about You. May my choices reflect Your character. May my life be marked with love.*

*I surrender my life to You, Lord—every moment of my day, each decision I make, I yield my will and way to Your perfect will and way. I commit to walking in Your way.*

*I love You too. Amen.*

# Rest, Catch Up, or Dig Deeper

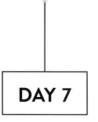 **WEEKLY CHALLENGE**

When we studied Romans 13, we prayed for the people who are in authority over us. This week, commit to pray for them by name every day. Ask God to guide you toward any actions you could take to seek the welfare of your city.

# Romans 15–16

## Scripture to Memorize

If the Spirit of him who raised Jesus from the dead dwells in you, he who raised Christ Jesus from the dead will also give life to your mortal bodies through his Spirit who dwells in you.

Romans 8:11

## DAILY BIBLE READING

Day 1: Romans 15:1–13

Day 2: Romans 15:14–21

Day 3: Romans 15:22–33

Day 4: Romans 16:1–16

Day 5: Romans 16:17–27

Day 6: Psalm 117

Day 7: Catch-Up Day

Corresponds to Day 345 of *The Bible Recap*.

## WEEKLY CHALLENGE

See page 280 for more information.

# Romans 15:1–13

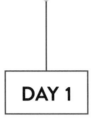 **READ ROMANS 15:1–13**

Keep in mind as we begin today that Romans is one continuous letter. The chapter and verse breaks weren't originally part of it; they were added at a later time for our benefit. So don't let the start of this new chapter make you think Paul has moved on to another topic. Instead, he continued his discussion about the "strong" and "weak" in faith (see 14:1–2).

**Review 15:1–2.**

By using the pronouns *we* and *us*, Paul placed himself in the category of "strong" in faith. (Remember, this meant freedom for Jewish Christians from the obligation of following the food laws.) Even though Paul aligned himself with this group, he didn't condemn the "weak." Instead, those who considered themselves strong had a greater responsibility in the relationship.

1. What did Paul instruct the "strong" believers to do in 15:1–2?

   A. Bear with the failings of the weak, not please ourselves, please our neighbors for their good, build them up

   B. Bear with the failings of the weak, please ourselves, build ourselves up

   C. Bear with the failings of the weak, assert ourselves, teach them what is right

   D. Bear with the failings of the weak, secretly judge them for their weak faith, pray that God changes their heart, build them up in public and tear them down in private

**Review 15:3–4.**

Christ served as an example of the attitude and actions Paul urged the Roman Christians to have toward each other. Jesus didn't come with a self-serving mindset—He came to love, serve, and minister to others, despite being mocked and disrespected.

Paul also highlighted the power of Scripture, which at this time was just the Old Testament, to help believers live as God desired.

★ 2. According to 15:4, what is the purpose of Scripture? What three things does it provide?

    A.

    B.

    C.

★ 3. Are there specific Old Testament passages that give you hope? If so, what are they?

**Review 15:5–7.**

With Christ as their example, Scripture for instruction, and God—who is the "God of endurance and encouragement"—Paul encouraged the Roman Christians to live in humility and unity despite their different opinions.

Paul cared deeply about the truth of the gospel. (You've studied fourteen chapters of Romans so far, so you know he had a few things to say about this!) But Paul was doing something different here. He addressed these important issues within the early church in humility and with a desire for unity within the body of Christ.

Remember, Christ brought together two radically different cultural, ethnic, and religious people groups—Jew and Gentile—to bring glory to God.

Some things were absolutes—all sin deserves punishment, only Christ justifies, Christians can never be separated from God's love. These were and are orthodox Christian beliefs.

But topics that weren't essential to the faith were open for believers to have different opinions on. Paul was adamant that Christians believed and lived according to the absolutes, *and* he gave freedom for the diversity of opinions.*

★ 4. What beliefs do you find yourself treating as absolutes when they're actually opinions? How does this affect your attitude and your interactions with others in your church or Christian community?

*For more information about the distinctions between absolutes, convictions, opinions, and questions, visit MyDGroup.org/beliefs.

Perhaps, when he wrote this section, Paul was thinking along the same lines of this popular quote: "In essentials, unity; in non-essentials, liberty; in all things, charity."[1]

**Review 15:7–12.**

Paul instructed the Roman Christians to welcome one another—once again using Christ as an example.

In His earthly ministry, Christ came to serve the Jews (Matthew 10:5–6, 15:24)—this fulfilled the promises God made in the Old Testament about the Messiah. But the plan was never to stop there. The Gentiles were always meant to be included in God's incredible plan of salvation (Romans 1:16).

This led to hope, because the promises were fulfilled in Scripture, and praise for God's truthfulness and mercy.

5. **Read the Old Testament verses quoted in 15:9–12.** In the four columns on the right, note the relevant words found in the passages.

| Quoted Old Testament Verse | Romans Verse | His People (Jews) | Praise | Gentiles | Hope |
|---|---|---|---|---|---|
| Psalm 18:49 | "Therefore I will praise you among the Gentiles, and sing to your name." | | | | |
| Deuteronomy 32:43 | "Rejoice, O Gentiles, with his people." | | | | |
| Psalm 117:1–2 | "Praise the Lord, all you Gentiles, and let all the peoples extol him." | | | | |
| Isaiah 11:1 | "The root of Jesse will come, even he who arises to rule the Gentiles; in him will the Gentiles hope." | | | | |

**Review 15:13.**

Previously, Paul referred to God as "the God of endurance and encouragement." Here, he referred to God as "the God of hope." Look back at the three things Scripture provided in 15:4 (Hint: You answered this question above).

Not only is God the God of endurance, encouragement, and hope, but He also *gives* endurance, encouragement, and hope through His Word.

# Romans 15:14–21

 **READ ROMANS 15:14–21**

**Review 15:14–15.**

In the last few sections, Paul's words might have come across as harsh or overly critical to his Roman audience. But here, we see his tone and heart shining through. He hoped to visit these believers, even though he hadn't played a role in establishing or leading the churches in Rome. He knew many of the believers there (we'll get to that in Romans 16), but he hadn't made it to visit them yet.

The things he knew about their faith and areas of struggle were likely based on their reputation, including any reports he might have heard. Paul was pleased with how well the believers were doing and took time to express his approval.

1. What three things did he mention about the Roman church in 15:14?

    A.

    B.

    C.

"Full of goodness" implied his audience demonstrated their faith and belief in Christ by honoring God—bearing fruit of righteousness—through the power of the Spirit.

Paul didn't write this letter because the Roman Christians needed theological correction. And although he provided some new teaching by addressing potential issues within the church, this also wasn't the reason he wrote. Instead, he said he just wanted to remind them of a few things.

We learned yesterday that one of the purposes of Scripture is instruction, which provides endurance, encouragement, and hope. Here, we see another powerful purpose of Scripture: It's a *reminder*. God's Word reminds us of His truth, character, love, and plan for salvation.

★ 2. Reflect on your study of Romans so far. Fill in the table below answering where you learned something new and where Scripture served as a reminder.

| I learned . . . | I was reminded . . . | Chapter and verse |
|---|---|---|
|  |  |  |
|  |  |  |
|  |  |  |

**Review 15:16.**

3. Read Isaiah 66:20 below. Circle the words or ideas that relate to Romans 15:16.

"And they shall bring all your brothers from all the nations as an offering to the LORD, on horses and in chariots and in litters and on mules and on dromedaries, to my holy mountain Jerusalem, says the LORD, just as the Israelites bring their grain offering in a clean vessel to the house of the LORD."

As we learned in Romans 12, the Old Testament sacrificial system no longer applied under the new covenant. Yet once again, Paul used language his audience would understand. Here, he applied sacrificial language to God's work, through Paul, among the Gentiles. "The nations" (Gentiles) were always on God's heart. God's desire—recorded in Isaiah—was ultimately implemented through Jesus and continued through His apostles and the early church.

**Review 15:17–20.**

The moment Paul met Jesus on the road to Damascus (see Acts 9:1–19), the entire trajectory of his life changed. Everything in his life reoriented around the person and work of Christ Jesus.

4. Write down the two phrases in 15:17–18 that demonstrate this.

Paul was proud of the work he did and shared freely about his ministry to the Gentiles (including commenting on the impact and geographical scope). He felt this freedom only because he was certain it was Christ at work in him—by the power of the Spirit of God—that produced anything of value in his ministry.

★ 5. Consider your understanding of God's work (Father, Son, and Spirit) in and through you. Where are you inclined to think you can take credit for the good work you do in your ministry, job, church, or community? Where are you inclined to think God is not at work in you? Explain.

In 15:19–20, Paul mentioned where he previously focused his efforts and his continued desire to share the gospel with those who hadn't heard it.

**6. Look at the map below and find Jerusalem and the region of Illyricum. Draw one circle that encompasses both places.**

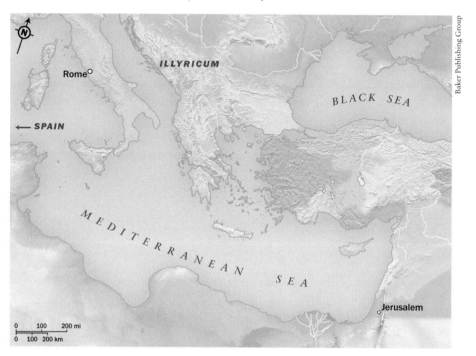

The book of Acts recorded Paul's three missionary journeys. Here, Paul hit the highlights—the gospel was preached, miracles happened, and Gentiles came to faith—all by the power of the Spirit of God.

Illyricum, a Roman province, wasn't explicitly mentioned during Paul's travels in Acts, although it's certainly possible he made it there. It's also possible he meant something like, *"I made it as far as the border of Illyricum"* (because he spent time in Macedonia). The scope of Paul's ministry covered about 1,400 miles—an astonishing distance at that time, revealing just how deeply he loved God and people.

Paul had an unrelenting desire to share the good news of Christ. This came from his understanding of the faithfulness of God—seen through Jesus—toward the Jewish people and ultimately toward the Gentiles and anyone who had yet to hear.

# Romans 15:22–33

 **READ ROMANS 15:22-33**

**Review 15:22–23.**

★ 1. Look back at yesterday's study. In your own words, explain why Paul hadn't made it to Rome yet.

Paul wasn't saying he had shared the gospel with every single person from Jerusalem to Illyricum. His role as an apostle ("sent-out one") meant he was called to preach, teach, establish churches, and appoint elders. Then he would move on to different cities and start again. Paul longed to tell everyone about Jesus. Therefore, he was compelled to travel westward to other regions that hadn't heard the good news yet.

**Review 15:24–25.**

2. On the map, circle Corinth, Paul's location when writing this letter. Then use three different colors or types of lines to mark his desired journey.

    A. Draw a line from Corinth to Jerusalem.

    B. Draw a line from Jerusalem to Rome.

    C. Draw a line from Rome to Spain. (*Hint: The most common route was by boat.*)

**Review 15:26–27.**

Before Paul could visit Rome he planned to go to Jerusalem. The church in Jerusalem—consisting of Jewish Christians—was struggling financially. To address this need, Paul encouraged the churches in Macedonia and Achaia—consisting of Gentile Christians—to provide assistance.

3. Circle the regions of Macedonia and Achaia on the map.

Yes, the Gentiles were happy to help, but it also sounds like they were "volun-told." And in reality they might have been. Paul was adamant about unity between Jewish and Gentile believers, and he knew that Israel's disobedience meant the gospel spread among Gentiles (11:11–12).

★ 4. Paul had many people who were influential in his life and ministry. Perhaps you've known people like that too. What person, ministry, or church has contributed significantly to your relationship with the Lord?

**Review 15:28–29.**

Paul felt so strongly about the importance of this financial gift that he planned to go out of his way—remember, he was trying to get to Rome—to deliver it himself. The trip from Corinth to Jerusalem was eight hundred miles.

As we've seen throughout this letter, Paul understood that nothing good that he did came from his own power or strength. Although he planned and prepared, he knew that only the "blessing of Christ" could get him to Rome.

**Review 15:30–33.**

At the beginning of Paul's letter he mentioned his prayers for the Roman Christians and his desire to see them. Here, Paul asked them to "strive together" with him in prayer for *him*. We might be inclined to think of Paul as a lone ranger—spreading the gospel around the world by himself. But this is far from the truth. He knew he needed prayer for what was ahead, and he wanted his friends in Rome to pray with him.

5. What are the three prayer requests in 15:31–32?

A.

B.

C.

The words *strive together* indicate an intense struggle. Perhaps Paul had in mind the struggle of the flesh to align our prayers with God's will. Most likely he meant that prayer can be a difficult—though rewarding—endeavor. It requires focus, determination, and stamina.

There was potential for uncertainty and peril as Paul embarked on his proposed journey. The "unbelievers in Judea"—the Jewish leaders—had persecuted Jewish Christians in the area and could pose a threat to Paul. Travel was also dangerous, and he planned to cover thousands of miles. In light of all this, Paul urged the Roman Christians to struggle alongside him in prayer.

6. Is there someone who needs your prayers? Write their initials below. Commit to struggling alongside them in prayer this week.

Throughout Romans 15, Paul commented on who God is: the God of endurance, encouragement, and hope. And here, he adds one more: the God of peace. No matter the outcome of Paul's proposed journey to Jerusalem, Rome, and Spain, he believed the God of peace would be with him. And he prayed the same for his friends in Rome.

# Romans 16:1–16

 **READ ROMANS 16:1-16**

If you've read Romans before, or even if you haven't, you might have been inclined to skim or even skip this section. (And if you skimmed or skipped it now, go back and read it.) There is encouragement we can glean from Paul's greetings to the believers in Rome.

**Review 16:1–2.**

First up, Phoebe.

1. Circle the words used to describe Phoebe.

    Sister

    Gentile

    Servant

    Christian

    Patron

    Fellow worker

Phoebe was responsible for delivering this letter (the book of Romans) to the believers in the city. Cenchreae, her hometown, was a port of Corinth. Paul followed the typical pattern of letter writing in the first century, which included a commendation. He introduced Phoebe, praised her service for the Lord, and encouraged the believers to be hospitable and generous toward her.

★ 2. **Look up** *servant* **(16:1) in a Greek lexicon and write the definition below. Read 16:1 in the NLT and NIV.** What word do these translations use instead of *servant*?

Some scholars believe Phoebe served in the formal role of deacon within her church.* It's hard to know for sure if this was Paul's meaning; however, it's clear Phoebe was trusted and respected by Paul and by those she served—whether formally or informally—in her ministry.

**Review 16:3–5a.**

Prisca—short for Priscilla—and Aquila were Paul's friends from his first visit to Corinth during his second missionary journey.

It's worth noting a few things about this New Testament power couple. Prisca and Aquila most likely helped Paul start the church in Corinth; Paul's reference to them as "fellow workers" implied they worked closely with him in ministry.

*See 1 Timothy 3:8–13 and https://www.gotquestions.org/deacons-church.html for information about deacons.

3. Fill in the profile for Prisca and Aquila. **Use 16:3–5 plus Acts 18:1–3, Acts 18:18–19, and Acts 18:24–26 as your guide.**

| | |
|---|---|
| **Name:** Priscilla | **Name:** Aquila |
| **Gender:** Female | **Gender:** Male |
| **Nickname:** | **Nickname:** none known |
| **Verses where name listed first in the pair:** | **Verses where name listed first in the pair:** Acts 18:2 |
| **Reason for leaving Rome:** | |
| **Profession:** | |
| **Relationship to Paul:** | |
| **Address of current church:** | |
| **Role in current church:** | |

There are a variety of opinions as to why Prisca's name was mentioned first in this section (and in Acts 18:18, 26 and 2 Timothy 4:19). Some think she was originally from Rome and perhaps held a higher social status than Aquila. Others note she might have been the more well-known teacher between the two. Regardless of Paul's reason, he clearly valued the friendship, leadership, courage, and devotion of Prisca and Aquila.

**Review 16:5b–16.**

There are twenty-nine people listed in 16:1–16. These names, greetings, and descriptions demonstrate the beauty and diversity within the body of Christ. The believers in Rome met in one another's homes to worship Christ. These house churches consisted of men and women (eight mentioned by name), Gentile believers, Jewish believers (referred to as kinsmen), servants, wealthy and prominent individuals, and those who had been imprisoned for the gospel.

Paul described some as hard workers, noted others' long-standing relationship with Christ, and recognized all of them as integral to the body of

Christ—which compelled him to greet them by name. Perhaps one of the reasons Paul so desperately wanted to visit Rome was to see some of his friends! Clearly these individuals were important to Paul, both personally and for the sake of the gospel.

★ 4. Write down three descriptions from this section that stand out to you and explain why.

A.

B.

C.

The good news of salvation—found only in Jesus Christ—was first heard in Jerusalem about twenty years before Paul wrote this letter. In that short time, the gospel traveled throughout Judea and Samaria, to Gentile regions in Asia and Europe, and made it all the way to Rome (following the order described in Acts 1:8). These individuals were some of the many who had heard and responded to God's call. Paul considered them to be his ministry partners and his family in Christ, and he couldn't wait to see them.

DAY 5

# Romans 16:17–27

 **READ ROMANS 16:17-27**

It sounded like Paul was concluding his letter in verse 16 with the "holy kiss" and the *"We say hi too!"* from the other churches in the Roman empire. But this mention of unity and familial love inspired him to make one final point: Be on the lookout for those who will disrupt unity within the body of Christ.

**Review 16:17–18.**

Paul's language of "appeal" and "watch out" demonstrated a strong warning for the believers to be on their guard against false teachers. In some of Paul's other letters—such as Galatians and Philippians—false teachers presented a clear and present danger within the churches. His warning here was more general, outlining the kinds of people false teachers were and why.

1. Using your own words, fill in the flowchart below.

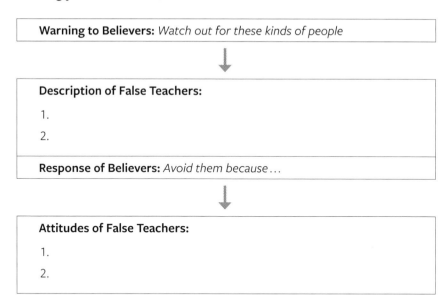

**Warning to Believers:** *Watch out for these kinds of people*

**Description of False Teachers:**

1.

2.

**Response of Believers:** *Avoid them because...*

**Attitudes of False Teachers:**

1.

2.

**Review 16:19.**

The obedience of the believers in Rome to God's truth was evident to Paul. Their reputation preceded them. He had already commended them for their moral excellence, knowledge, and ability to teach one another (15:14). Yet Paul encouraged them to continue in their pursuit of goodness by growing in wisdom.

Wisdom—knowing and applying God's truth—would fortify them against the manipulation of false teachers.

Knowledge of God's Word, and the proper application of it, protects all believers from deception. Good news: You have already been applying this principle! Throughout these last ten weeks, by engaging in this study, you've been actively growing in what is good and protecting yourself from lies and deception.

★ 2. Write down two truths you've learned about God through this study.

A.

B.

**Review 16:20.**

Paul previously described God as "the God of peace" (15:33), and here we see an interesting action associated with His peace: crushing Satan.

Paul referenced Genesis 3:14–15, which theologians refer to as the *protevangelium*—a foreshadowing of the gospel. All the way back in Genesis, immediately after Adam and Eve sinned, God promised salvation. Jesus would deal with sin and Satan, the original false teacher.

We all wait with anticipation for Jesus's return—when sin, Satan, death, and all evil will be defeated once for all. And, as Paul reminded his audience, we do have a role to play while we wait. We actively participate in overcoming evil by living holy lives; pursuing truth, righteousness, peace, and joy; and demonstrating wisdom in knowing and living according to God's Word.

3. Look back at the truths you wrote above. How do these truths practically impact the way you live? Briefly explain.

A.

B.

**Review 16:21–23.**

These eight men partnered with Paul in his ministry and were with him in Corinth when he wrote this letter. Tertius, Paul's scribe, even gave himself a shout-out. (We're certainly thankful you wrote this down, Tertius!)

Once again the diversity within the early church was evident. Paul's companions included Jews (kinsmen), Gentiles, people with high social status, and people who used their gifts for hospitality. All labored diligently in their work for Christ alongside Paul.

**Review 16:25–27.***

4. Fill in the chart using your own words. Enjoy the glorious conclusion, Paul's final doxology in his letter to the Romans.

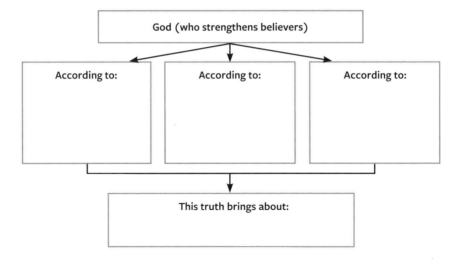

God's plan of salvation, established in eternity and revealed through Scripture, is for our good and His glory. He's where the joy is!

---

*In some translations, 16:24 has been omitted. This part of the text wasn't included in some earlier manuscripts, which is why it is absent here. Later manuscripts that include it have been translated to say, "The grace of our Lord Jesus Christ be with you all. Amen."

5. What stood out to you most in this week's study? Why?

6. What did you learn or relearn about God and His character this week?

**DAY 6**

# Corresponding Psalm & Prayer

 **READ PSALM 117**

1. What correlation do you see between Psalm 117 and this week's study?

2. What portions of this psalm stand out to you most?

3. Close by praying this prayer aloud:

*Father,*
*    Your steadfast love is great, and Your faithfulness endures forever.*
*You set Israel apart for the sake of the whole world, and through*

*Your Son, I get to join with people from all nations in the chorus: Praise the Lord!*

*While You have built a beautifully diverse kingdom, I have failed to honor that beauty, insisting that my opinions are Your absolutes. I've sought to please myself, and I haven't built up my neighbor. Stop me from doing any damage to my fellow heirs in Your kingdom.*

*Thank You for giving the saints of the early church faithfulness in sharing Your good news with the nations. The gospel made its way to me, like You always knew it would! Lead me, and my fellow saints today, in faithfulness. May we always share Your good news with the nations. May we be diligent in building Your kingdom.*

*I surrender my life to You, Lord—every moment of my day, each decision I make, I yield my will and way to Your perfect will and way.*

*I love You too. Amen.*

DAY 7

# Rest, Catch Up, or Dig Deeper

### ✝ WEEKLY CHALLENGE

Look back to Day 3's fourth prompt, where you wrote down the person, ministry, or church that contributed significantly to your relationship with the Lord. This week, show your appreciation for them by writing a thank-you note, taking them to lunch, donating to their ministry, or volunteering.

# FOR GROUP LEADERS

Thank you for using this study and leading others through it as well! Each week has a wide variety of content (daily Bible reading, content and questions, Scripture memorization, weekly challenge, and resources) to help the reader develop a range of spiritual disciplines. Feel free to include as much or as little of that in your meetings as you'd like. The details provided in How to Use This Study (pp. 9–11) will be helpful to you and all your group members, so be sure to review that information together!

It's up to you and your group how you'd like to structure your meetings, but we suggest including time for discussion of the week's study and Bible text, mutual encouragement, and prayer. You may also want to practice your Scripture memory verses together as a group or in pairs. As you share with each other, "consider how to stir up one another to love and good works" (Hebrews 10:24) and "encourage one another and build one another up" (1 Thessalonians 5:11).

Here are some sample questions to help facilitate discussion. This is structured as a weekly study, but if your group meets at a different frequency, you may wish to adjust the questions accordingly. Cover as many questions as time allows, or feel free to come up with your own. And don't forget to check out the additional resources we've linked for you at MyDGroup.org/Resources/Romans.

## Sample Discussion Questions

What questions did this week's study or Bible text bring up for you?

What stood out to you in this week's study?

What did you notice about God and His character?

How were you challenged by your study of the Bible text? Is there anything you want to change in light of what you learned?

How does what you learned about God affect the way you live in community?

What correlation did you see between the psalm from Day 6 and this week's study of Romans?

Have you felt God working in you through the weekly challenge? If so, how?

Is your love for God's Word increasing as we go through this study? If so, how?

Did anything you learned increase your joy in knowing Jesus?

# ACKNOWLEDGMENTS

Laura Buchelt, Emily Pickell, Abbey Dane, Emma Dotter, Kirsten Mc-Closkey, and Liz Suggs—thank you for your incredible research, creativity, wisdom, humility, and laughter. It's truly a *blast* to study God's Word with you all!

Olivia Le—thank you for making our writing summits so seamless and for bringing levity to our lunches.

Lisa Jackson—you continue to be such a gift as a guide, agent, and friend.

And to the rest of the incredible D-Group Team—Rachel Mantooth, Lindsay Ruhter, Warwick Fuller, Meg Mitchell, Evaline Asmah, and our board, leaders, members, and church partners around the world—I love being on mission with you!

# NOTES

**Introduction**

1. *Luther's Small Catechism with Explanation* (Concordia Publishing House, 2011), 97.

**Week 1: Day 5**

1. Ligonier Editorial, "The Threefold Use of the Law," Ligonier, August 21, 2015, https://www.ligonier.org/learn/articles/threefold-use-law.

**Week 2: Day 2**

1. Warren W. Wiersbe, *Be Right: An Expository Study of Romans* (Victor Books, 1983), 31.

**Week 2: Day 3**

1. Quoted in F. F. Bruce, *The Epistle of Paul to the Romans: An Introduction and Commentary* (Wm. B. Eerdmans Publishing Company, 1963), 59.
2. Timothy Keller, *Romans 1–7 for You* (The Good Book Company, 2014), 92.

**Week 3: Day 4**

1. Thomas Fuller, *Good Thoughts in Bad Times and Other Papers* (University Press: Welch, Bigelow, and Company, 1863), https://www.ccel.org/ccel/fuller/goodthoughts.iv.iii.xi.html.

**Week 4: Day 2**

1. Net Bible, Constable's Notes on Romans 7:6, https://netbible.org/bible/Romans+7#.

**Week 10: Day 1**

1. Rupert Meldenius quoted in John Stott, *Romans: God's Good News for the World* (Intervarsity Press, 1994), 375.

# ABOUT THE EDITOR

**TARA-LEIGH COBBLE'S** various ministries are all focused on helping people read, understand, and love God's Word. Her zeal for biblical literacy led her to create a network of Bible studies called D-Group (Discipleship Group) International. Every week, hundreds of men's and women's D-Groups meet in homes, in churches, and online for Bible study and accountability.

She also writes and hosts a daily podcast called *The Bible Recap* designed to help listeners read, understand, and love the Bible in a year. The podcast garnered over four hundred million downloads, and more than twenty thousand churches around the world have joined their reading plan to know and love God better. It has been turned into a book published by Bethany House Publishers.

Tara-Leigh is a *Wall Street Journal* bestselling author, speaks to a wide variety of audiences, and regularly leads teaching trips to Israel because she loves to watch others be awed by the story of Scripture through firsthand experience.

Her favorite things include sparkling water and days that are 72 degrees with 55 percent humidity, and she thinks every meal tastes better when eaten outside. She lives in a concrete box in the skies of Dallas, Texas, where she has no pets, children, or anything that might die if she forgets to feed it.

For more information about Tara-Leigh and her ministries, you can visit her online.

Websites: taraleighcobble.com | thebiblerecap.com | mydgroup.org | israelux.com
Social media: @taraleighcobble | @thebiblerecap | @mydgroup | @israeluxtours